YOKED

Teaching Apprentices of Jesus

Larry K. Asplund

ISBN: 978-0-692-18845-3

Dr. Asplund has written an insightful commentary on the commandments of Jesus in the book of Matthew. It is written with the richness of personal reflection, intuitive study and inspirational insights. The reader will be freshly enlightened into the truths presented in the Gospel of Matthew and find it to be a good resource for continued study into this great Gospel text.

Glenda Malmin
Dean of Women / Professor of Theology
Portland Bible College
Portland, Oregon

We live in a culture that defines freedom as having no restraints. In contrast, the Scriptures make clear that the only way to be truly free is to be bound or "yoked" to Jesus Christ and his word. In this book, Dr. Asplund explores what it means to be yoked to Jesus Christ as his disciple. He explores the Gospel of Matthew and its simple commands as a very practical guide to embrace the essentials of discipleship—the very attitudes and actions that make us Christian and different from the world. Whether you are looking for a spiritual tune up or need a complete spiritual overhaul, this book is indispensable.

Dr. James T. Flynn
Associate Dean
Regent University
Virginia Beach, Virginia

Yoked is an engaging exploration of how to live as a genuine disciple of Christ. Larry expertly guides us through the commands of Jesus in his sermons throughout the Gospel of Matthew. More than enlightenment, the outcome is encouragement to walk closely with Christ. This is a fantastic resource for both personal growth and group study.

Travis Arnold
Professor
Portland Bible College
Portland, Oregon

It is with highest honor that I can recommend this book, "Yoked" by Dr. Larry Asplund. First of all, Dr. Asplund writes with the credentials of a seasoned and compassionate leader. Secondly, he is a wonderful scholar mining the scriptures in ways that will bring revelation and fresh insight to the reader. Lastly, and most importantly, Dr. Asplund models genuine humility in all things and writes from a shepherd's heart to see people truly understand the blessing of living a "Yoked" life!   I believe those mature in the Lord and novices alike will find this book a useful tool and guide toward a greater pursuit of Jesus' teachings. May you discover in "Yoked" that the commands of Jesus are not burdensome, but rather easy to be entreated, understood and lived out in daily victory by His followers. Well done Dr. Larry Asplund. Thank you for blessing people with this work!

Dr. Randal S. Langley, President
Christian Life School of Theology Global
Pensacola, Florida

Dr. Larry Asplund has been a long-time pastoral colleague, mentor, and friend and I have benefited greatly from his wealth of scriptural knowledge. I was blessed to be present at the beginning stages of this incredible work as Larry and I explored the yoked life together. What has transpired in the pages of this book is perhaps one of the most important works in the area of Christian discipleship as Larry thoroughly presents the commands of Jesus shared throughout the gospel of Matthew. Dr. Asplund has written a is an excellent resource for personal study, private devotion and practical spiritual development for those dedicated to becoming fully devoted apprentices of Jesus.

Dr. J. Lamar Hardwick, Lead Pastor
New Community Church
Lagrange, Georgia

Dedication

My go-to editor has always been my wife. I was hoping she would be able to edit this book, but she passed into God's Glory as I was completing the final chapter, having been very sick for several months. I dedicate this book to my wife, best friend and ministry partner of 47 years, Lynda Kay Sutton Asplund, May 18, 1947, to June 29, 2018.

CONTENTS

Acknowledgments

I want to say a special "Thank you" to those dear friends who made this book possible by encouraging me to finish the work during a very difficult season. My dear friend and colleague, Dr. Marsha Rano, seeing that my precious wife was no longer available to edit, graciously offered to do the editing for me. Among other things, Marsha has served as an author and professional editor and gave the manuscript expert attention. Leah Watts, one of my favorite local artists, applied her amazing creative genius to the cover design. Thank you to my friend and Pastor, Dr. Lamar Hardwick, who appears in the Preface as the partner in ministry who team-taught the original sermon series that gave birth to this book. PastorL has the honor of leading a wonderful congregation in Lagrange, Georgia, New Community Church, my Georgia family. I love you, NCC! And a very special thanks goes to the members of my family. My daughter Charity and my son James have been stalwart personal supporters during these days. And my parents, Ken and Norma Asplund, have always been a great and consistent source of encouragement to whatever I think I might want to do; thank you, Mom and Dad. May this study represent the King well and be a source of blessing and encouragement to those who read it.

PREFACE

We were trying to find our way – the way that would take us out of our discouragement and confusion and into the future God had in mind for us as a congregation. Our pastor — and my friend — had just resigned in the midst of controversy. At the same time, my wife's heart became very weak as a result of a dangerous blockage, requiring surgery. Our pastoral leadership team was holding together, seeking the Lord.

That's when the image came to our minds of the "yoke" used to enable two oxen to work together. Jesus had invited his followers to take his yoke upon them and to learn of him. No matter what the future might hold for us, it seemed certain that the way forward was under the yoke of Jesus. And so, we launched into a message series we simply called, "The Jesus Way." Another staff pastor and I shared in a long (18 week) series that explored the "yoked life" Jesus was calling all of us to live, corporately and individually.

Part of the series explored the "Great Commission" as recorded in Matthew's Gospel. Jesus left his followers with clear instructions: They were to make disciples by teaching people to obey all he had commanded them. I don't know about you, but I've never really thought about Jesus as giving commandments. We all know about the Ten Commandments in the book of Exodus, but Jesus came "full of grace." Surely fullness of grace did not involve commandments, let alone the need to obey those commandments. But there it was, recorded plainly in these famous words of Jesus.

When we finally finished our series, I began a personal follow-up study of the "commandments" of Jesus as recorded in Matthew's Gospel. If making (and being) disciples requires us to teach people how to obey the commandments of Jesus, maybe we should focus more attention on what those commandments are, and how to obey them. I decided to dust off my old Greek grammar and do a study on every time Jesus used the "imperative mood" in his teaching as recorded in the gospel of Matthew. Since the imperative mood implies the authority of the one using it, this seemed like a helpful starting point.

It's important to remember that the idea of "commandments" in the Bible is broader than the way we normally use the word. A "commandment" is more than a rule or requirement. A biblical "commandment" is intended to provide teaching and guidance on how to live under the authority of God. In the Old Testament, *Torah* is the word, usually translated "law," that describes the instruction of God concerning the way of life designed for God's people under the covenant. The exploration of the "commands" of Jesus needs to be seen in this larger context – they are the authoritative teachings of Jesus intended to show us how to live under his "yoke."

I was determined to take another look at the sermons in Matthew's Gospel and at the uses of the imperative mood throughout the Gospel. My goal was simple: (1) To explore in greater detail the "commands" of Jesus, and in the process, (2) To explore what a life of obedience to those commands might involve.

Matthew's presentation of the teaching of Jesus is particularly helpful. His gospel provides us with five "sermons" or topically-related groupings of teaching. Since the vast majority of imperatives used by Jesus are in these sermons, I wanted to take a fresh look at their importance to our understanding of the "yoked life" as well as other important imperatives in the teaching of Jesus.

The result is the book you have before you.

In chapter one I will explore what "the yoked life" is all about, especially in light of Matthew's account of the Great Commission. "The Sermon on the Mount" will then be our focus. Because of its significance two chapters will be devoted to its consideration: part one (Matthew 5) in chapter 2, and part two (Matthew 6-7) in chapter 3. I then noticed several places where Jesus commanded his followers to "believe," commenting on the role of faith in obeying him and the all-too frequent instances of little faith. This will be the focus of chapter 4.

The second "sermon" is found in Matthew 10, the area of my exploration in chapter 5. I will explore the many times Jesus commanded those following him to receive salvation, healing and deliverance – the topic of chapter 6.

Matthew's third "sermon" is found in chapter 13 of the Gospel, a beautiful and profoundly important collection of Kingdom parables – the focus of chapter 7. The fourth sermon in Matthew (18) is what I call the "Sermon on the Church," providing principles and promises for the church Jesus is building – the focus of chapter 8. Jesus often commanded his followers to "be awake," to "be alert," and to "watch and pray," the subject of chapter 9. The fifth and final sermon is the "Sermon on the End" (Matthew 23-25), made up of two parts that describe the judgment coming on the generation of Jesus' day as well as final judgment. Chapter 10 will explore those important teachings of Jesus.

I have not attempted to write a commentary on the Gospel of Matthew. In fact, most of the Gospel of Matthew remains unexplored by this book. My purpose in writing is narrowly focused on the "commands" of Jesus and our need to make disciples by teaching them how to obey those commands. I have highlighted every case of an imperative command by making it bold.

So why would you be interested in reading this book?

1.   If you are a fully devoted follower of Jesus, you are dedicated to hearing and obeying whatever he might say to you.

2.   If you are not currently a Jesus follower but are curious about his teachings and their potential relevance to your life, you might be interested in exploring those teachings.

3.   If you love the Scriptures, the Gospels, and the Gospel of Matthew in particular, you will relish the beauty of Matthew's presentation.

4.   If you are a pastor or teacher and are interested in a teaching tool, you might find this book useful.

I have chosen to write more informally and conversationally, as if I were teaching this material in a live classroom, not using an "academic" voice but an adult Bible study voice. However, I have greatly benefited down through the years by a variety of excellent resources, all of which I am willing to recommend. Here is a short list:

I devoured "The Cost of Discipleship" by Dietrich Bonhoeffer, as a young believer, and still find it relevant today. John R. W. Stott's "Sermon on the Mount" is another great introduction to those chapters in Matthew. The wonderful sermon series, "Studies in the Sermon on the Mount," by D. Martyn Lloyd-Jones is a master piece. If you love commentaries, I can recommend "The Gospel of Matthew, by R. T. France, the two-volume "Expositor's Bible Commentary" on Matthew by D. A.

Carson, the Exegetical Commentary on the New Testament's volume on "Matthew" by Grant R. Osborne, and the more recent work by Craig S. Keener, "The Gospel of Matthew: A Socio-Rhetorical Commentary."

My sincere prayer for you as you read this study is not only for clear and helpful understanding but also for a new zeal to join Jesus under his yoke, allowing his life and teachings to guide you every step of the way.

Larry K. Asplund

1 THE YOKED LIFE

People tend to be fascinated with the "last words" spoken by a person, especially a famous person. Somehow, we think that such a profound moment as a person's passing from this life to the next must involve something amazing and insightful being spoken. It's fairly easy to find a list of "famous last words," some quite surprising. While they aren't always profound, they often reveal something about the person speaking them.

"This is the last of earth! I am content" (President John Quincy Adams).

"I am ready to die for my Lord, that in my blood the Church may obtain liberty and peace" (Thomas a Becket).

"Beautiful" (Elizabeth Barrett Browning).

"I must go in, the fog is rising" (Emily Dickenson).

"It is very beautiful over there" (Thomas Edison).

"I am ready" (President Woodrow Wilson).

"See in what peace a Christian can die" (Joseph Addison).

"Now comes the mystery" (Henry Ward Beecher).

"I should never have switched from Scotch to Martinis" (Humphrey Bogart).

"I'm bored with it all" (Winston Churchill).

We are particularly interested in the "last words" of Jesus. Obviously, Jesus never spoke "last words" since Jesus is still alive and is still speaking today. However, his final words to his followers gave very specific instructions and promises that are still relevant today. Every time I read them it's as though Jesus is speaking personally and directly to you and me.

We will begin our exploration of the "commands" of Jesus by examining these "last words" and the final "commission" of Jesus. But first, let's set the scene...

The Command to *Take* and *Eat*

I love how Jesus demonstrated his knowledge of and authority over his circumstances as he faced his last days. The Feast of Passover was approaching–a high point in the Jewish year. Jewish believers from all over the world would gather in Jerusalem to celebrate God's deliverance of Israel from Egypt all those centuries before. The Feast was always celebrated on the same day every year, on the 15th day of the month Nisan (not the Japanese car), also known as the month of Aviv, sometime during our months of March or April. This day was usually not on a Sabbath day, so both the Passover Feast day and the Passover Sabbath were celebrated, culminating in a celebration of the Feast of Firstfruits on the day after the Passover Sabbath. The Feast of Firstfruits celebrated the beginning of a new harvest season and the promise of a greater harvest to come. Jesus was about to give this festival cycle a whole new meaning.

Jesus led the disciples into a time of celebration with a clear and specific knowledge of its meaning, not only in Israel's history but also in his life and ministry, and in the future of his Kingdom community. The glory of the Father was about to be demonstrated – if they only had eyes to see.

It began with Jesus giving his disciples specific instructions on how to prepare for the celebration. "**Go** into the city to a certain man and **tell** him, 'The Teacher says: My appointed time is near. I am going to celebrate the Passover with my disciples at your house'" (26:18). Jesus spoke with authority, commanding the disciples to "go" and to "tell" a certain man about the need to prepare for the Passover. I suppose these instructions would not have been all that unusual for a Rabbi and his pupils. But Jesus had a unique perspective. "My appointed time is near." In the Greek language (change to present tense or add qualifier to language: "ancient" Greek...), there is more than one word for "time." The one we're most familiar with is "chronos," from which we get words like "chronology." It is simply linear time measured in seconds, minutes, hours, days, etc. There is another word we're less familiar with – "kairos," referring to a key moment in time, a turning point, a prophetic window, usually translated "set time" or "appointed time." This is the word Jesus used here. He understood that the appointed time – the time for

God's purpose to be fulfilled, the time for God's eternal love and redemption to be accomplished – was "near." It had arrived, it was upon them, it had come.

Jesus saw this moment in the light of God's eternal purpose. This was to be no ordinary Passover celebration. This Passover would deliver God's people from the bondage of human sin and set human history onto a whole new course. Because Jesus clearly saw the meaning of that moment in his life, he took control of the details. He was never surprised, never caught unprepared. He even knew who was to make space available for him and his disciples, beginning this profoundly important Passover.

It's interesting that Jesus referred to himself as "the Teacher." Jesus was their Rabbi, the disciple-maker. That's why verse 19 simply states that the disciples "did as Jesus had directed them." I think the word (Greek *suntasso*) translated "directed" in this verse is interesting: it means "to put in order with or together, to arrange." Jesus is literally organizing his disciples based on his understanding of the importance of that Passover celebration.

As the Passover meal began Jesus began with one of his "Amen sayings." When Jesus wanted to emphasize the absolute truthfulness of something as well as his authority to say it, he began by saying, "Amen, I say to you," or "Truly I tell you" (verse 21). Once again, Jesus is demonstrating his understanding of the time and his authority over the details of this situation.

As the Passover meal progressed Jesus came to the unique expressions of God's salvation, commanding the disciples to "take," to "eat," and to "drink." "While they were eating, Jesus took bread, and when he had given thanks, he broke it and gave it to his disciples, saying, '**Take** and **eat**; this is my body.' Then he took a cup, and when he had given thanks, he gave it to them, saying, '**Drink** from it, all of you. This is my blood of the covenant, which is poured out for many for the forgiveness of sins'" (26:26-28).

It was at this point in the Passover meal that the head of the family traditionally pronounced God's blessing with the bread and the wine. "Blessed art thou, O Lord our God, King of the universe, who bringest forth bread from the earth," the traditional blessing over the bread. And then with the cup, the third cup, the cup of blessing; "Blessed art thou, O Lord our God, King of the universe, Creator of the fruit of the vine." Only this time these words, and indeed the bread and the cup, were taking on new meaning. Jesus was revealing himself by "breaking bread" and "giving thanks" (from the Greek *eucharisteo*, from which we get our word "eucharist.") Jesus was making some rather radical statements about his body being broken and his blood being poured out. He referred to "the blood of the covenant" that was to be shed "for the forgiveness of sins."

I sometimes wonder how much the disciples really understood at that point. Jesus was initiating a new covenant and bringing in a new deliverance for God's people; not from Egypt but from sin, and ultimately from the curse, the consequences of sin, even death itself.

It's interesting that the traditional Jewish blessings refer to God as the "King of the universe," a very broad understanding of God's rule. At the end of the meal Jesus made a promise – he would ultimately celebrate this new Passover, this new covenant meal, "new...in my Father's kingdom" (verse 29).

Jesus was leading his clueless disciples on a very specific pathway to a new experience of salvation and a new life in God's Kingdom. And he was in control every step of the way, giving his followers and friends clear commandments to follow.

We can be confident that the Lord knows what he is doing in our lives. Our lives don't always make sense – in fact, sometimes it seems as though our lives are spinning out of control. That's when we may need to be reminded that Jesus knows what's going on in our lives, that Jesus is in control. We can listen for his specific instructions and be confident that as we hear and obey, he will lead us on to the Kingdom pathway, the way of salvation and blessing, he has purposed for our lives.

The path he was on would ultimately lead to his death – but that was not the end of the story. The Feast of Firstfruits was coming–Easter Sunday was on the way!

The Command to *Go* and *Tell*

The death of Jesus was not the end of the story – not by a long way. Jesus had been clear that "on the third day" he would rise from the dead, the "first fruits" of the resurrection (see 1 Corinthians 15:20, 23). As the sun was rising on that first Easter morning, the Son was also rising. When Matthew told the story, he recorded that Mary Magdalene and "the other Mary" were the first ones to return to the tomb. These are the same two women that had stayed with Jesus the entire time he was on the cross and accompanied his body to the tomb (Matthew 27:56, 61). As they arrived, Matthew states that a great earthquake occurred, and "an angel of the Lord" rolled back the stone from the entrance of the tomb and sat on it.

What an astounding and frightening experience that must have been! We read that the strong, well-trained guards were so afraid they literally shook and passed out. And for good reason! That's why the angel encouraged the women to not be afraid. Not only was Jesus no longer in the tomb, but he had also risen from the dead and the tomb was empty.

The angel then commissioned the women to go and announce the resurrection of Jesus to his disciples and to instruct them to go to Galilee where Jesus would meet them.

But that was not the end of their experience. As they were leaving, they met Jesus. Matthew's account tells of the women hurrying away from the tomb to bring the good news to the disciples in obedience to the angel's instructions. They were still afraid, but they were also filled with joy. They were prepared to believe everything the angel had told them and to announce it boldly to the disciples waiting in Jerusalem. But before they got very far, Jesus greeted them. The common "**Greetings**" is literally a command to "rejoice!" As you can imagine, the women were so overjoyed they fell down on the ground, grabbed hold of Jesus' feet and worshiped him. Their response was very visceral and physical. (Even the idea of "worship" means "to kiss the hand.") These women loved Jesus with all their hearts, and they poured out their love as they rejoiced and greeted their risen Lord.

Jesus then gave them some specific commands. First of all, he repeated the command of the angel (from verse 5): "**Do not be afraid**," or stop being afraid. It's amazing how many times we see Jesus commanding people to not fear. While fear can be a positive thing, as with "the fear of the Lord," it can also be a negative, paralyzing experience. Fear is an instinctive reaction to a potentially threatening or unknown situation. We sometimes call it a "fight, flight, or freeze" response. It has been rightly said that fear has the power to paralyze our faith. The arrest, trial, death, and burial of Jesus must have been a very frightening, discouraging, disorienting, traumatic experience for these women. And now they experience an earthquake, witness an angel roll the stone away from the entrance to the tomb, and then hear Jesus. It must have all been too much! But Jesus wants them to respond in faith, not just react in fear. They need to deal with their natural, overwhelming fear before they can really move on to the new reality Jesus has for them.

Jesus then gave the women two simple words of instruction: "**Go**" and "**tell**." They are to move from their position of worship, to let him go physically, and "go" to the disciples. When they arrive, they are to "tell," they are to officially announce to the disciples the good news that Jesus is alive. This is their personal commission, the responsibility given to them as official witnesses of the resurrection.

I love how Jesus refers to the disciples as "my brothers." You would think that the resurrected Lord would view himself as being far above these men, someone who is to be obeyed and worshiped as their Lord and God. And while that is certainly true, in this initial message Jesus thought of them as his brothers. He identified himself as the brother – the elder brother, the firstborn son – of his followers.

I also love how Jesus instructed them to meet him in Galilee. This was considered by the Jewish elite to be a despised area, filled with people who were less than "clean" or entirely orthodox. But the mission Jesus was about to send his brothers on was to be to all "nations." What better place to launch that mission than in Galilee.

Our Lord wants us to love him, to adore him, to pour out our hearts to him. He also wants us to be clear about the assignments he gives us along the way. There are specific instructions, specific acts of obedience we will be called on to make. Before giving us those instructions, Jesus will carefully attend to our hopes and fears. He will position us to respond to him with faith before giving us our "orders." He will then put us in the place that will allow us to see the big Kingdom picture and our role in it.

The Command to *Make Disciples*

After forty days with Jesus, the resurrected Lord, the time finally came for Jesus to give final instructions to his followers. We know from Paul that there were over 500 people in attendance (1 Corinthians 15:6). Jesus had gathered his followers one last time to clearly define their mission. Jesus did not just leave his friends with a promise that when they died, they would go to heaven. He left them with a Kingdom task. He would ask them to continue the same mission that had brought him from heaven to earth (John 20:21). While it is certainly true that Jesus brought God's salvation, he had established more than that. In the big picture, Jesus came as the King, and when he showed up, his royal right to rule came with him. Jesus established the domain of the king. Jesus was the King of God's Kingdom that had come to earth with his coming.

And so, the final instructions of Jesus described the Kingdom mission he was passing on to his followers. He left them with the commission to express the quality and nature of his rule and to extend the influence and reach of his rule, "on earth as it is in heaven."

All authority. The gospel of Matthew presents Jesus as the King and announces the Gospel of the Kingdom. For that reason, "authority" (Greek *exousia*) is one of the key words in Matthew (cf. 7:9; 8:9; 9:6, 8; 10:1; 21:23, 24, 27). The word meant the same then as it does for us now: power, ability, strength, influence, right, rule, government. Jesus came as God's designated representative, as the "one and only" Son of the Father–Creator, with full authority to establish God's rule on the earth. As a result of his coming, life, ministry, death, and resurrection, Jesus has "all authority."

There is no authority anywhere that does not belong to Jesus. Nothing escapes his influence and rule...

...in heaven and on earth. After humanity issued a declaration of independence in the Garden from the rule of God (Genesis 3), God moved the headquarters of his Kingdom to heaven. It is currently the place of God's throne, the center of God's rule. In fact, when referring to the Kingdom of God Matthew uses the phrase, "Kingdom of heaven." Jesus came from heaven, from God's throne, representing God's rule, and Jesus brought the authority of heaven to the earth. As a result, divine kingly authority centered in heaven at God's throne had been given to Jesus, who was now the Ruler of all the rulers of the earth (Revelation 1:5). With the coming of Christ, the Messianic Kingdom had come.

...has been given to me. There are several times in Matthew's gospel when we see a "divine passive," a statement where Jesus acknowledges that something had been given to him by God. It acknowledges that the primary actor is always behind the scene, the one who is truly in control. Jesus didn't give himself all authority. Jesus didn't snatch all authority away from the devil (who only thought he had it). All authority was given to him by the Father.

*Therefore...**make disciples***. And now we come to the central element of the commission, the crux of the matter, the essence of the mission Jesus is entrusting to his followers. The assignment being handed off to the disciples of Jesus is to reproduce themselves, to "make disciples." Making disciples begins with recruiting men and women to be apprentices of Jesus. A disciple is a student, a personal follower, someone who is committed to a teacher, to learning everything a teacher has to teach as well as learning the teacher's way of life.

"Making disciples" is first of all a relational mission, facilitating relationships between the teacher and his pupils. But the teacher/disciple relationship is not just personal, it is also a clear commitment to learn and to follow, to obey and to imitate. Disciples are those who hear, understand, and obey the instructions of Jesus.

Having a clear vision and mission statement along with core values is the foundation of strategic planning and has become very popular in the church today. For Jesus, it is very simple: the vision is to be a disciple-making people; the mission is to make disciples; the primary core value is to do whatever it takes to raise up authentic followers of Jesus. For some today the primary task of the church is to offer folks "fire insurance," to lead them in some kind of "sinner's prayer" and then announce that when they die they will go to heaven. Other congregations may view their mission as being "culturally relevant." Fortunately, a new generation of American pastors are clearly seeing that the mission is to make disciples, not just to fill up heaven with people but to raise up followers who will accurately represent the King and exercise the King's authority in our time and place.

...of all nations. What has been implied throughout Matthew's gospel is now made clear: the mission of the Messiah is no longer ethnic, it is universal. Disciples are to be recruited and trained from all "nations." When you see this word, don't think of a modern nation-state. This is the word (Greek *ethne*) for people groups, ethnic groups. Disciples are to be raised up in every culture, every tribe, every language group on the face of the earth. Every boundary is to be crossed, every culture is to be bridged, in the process of making disciples.

...go...baptizing...and teaching. Within the context of the commandment to "make disciples" Jesus gives three very important words of instruction connected to the overall command. In passing on heaven's Kingdom mission Jesus tells his followers to "go." It was not the intent of Jesus to command potential disciples to "come." Jesus expected his committed followers to go, to recruit and train apprentices in the culture, in the surrounding society. The modern church may seek to create a warm inviting church atmosphere, to offer an attractive menu of religious goods and services, and then send the invitations out into the community to "come." I think some church leaders actually believe that "if you build it, they will come." Doing so does not achieve the mission. Every follower is expected to go, into whatever life circumstance God has placed them, and make disciples.

...baptizing them in the name of the Father and of the Son and of the Holy Spirit. It's not possible to make disciples without going. When we see the meaning and nature of the mission of God we will clearly see the need to go. But then we have to ask, "Go

and do what?" Jesus summarizes the process of disciple-making with two words: "baptizing" and "teaching."

"Baptism" has been called the primary sacrament of initiation in the Christian faith. It is the "sign" of the new covenant (functioning like circumcision did for the old covenant). It is the outward way we Jesus followers indicate our true inward faith in Jesus and our heart-felt commitment to following, obeying, and representing him. In essence, the instruction concerning "baptizing" states the need to introduce people to Jesus, and to do it in such a way as to lead to a lifelong commitment as authentic disciples. This is the process of recruiting apprentices to Jesus, of providing an orientation to the lifestyle of following Jesus, of helping people connect to the Father's heart, and of entering into the abundant life available through Christ in the Kingdom of God.

For followers of Jesus, baptism is a sign both of our entrance into Messiah's covenant community as well as a pledge to submit to his authority as King. New recruits are to have more than a personal and private faith. They must be willing to publicly declare their complete identification with Jesus through baptism.

It's interesting that Jesus instructed his followers to baptize "in the name of the Father and of the Son and of the Holy Spirit." "In the name of" makes the symbol of baptism very personal. It means that the pledge of faith and obedience is not just an abstract idea but is rather a personal "loyalty oath" to God. It also means that God is directly and personally present, involved at this moment of public covenant-making. "In the name of" could be stated as "coming into relationship with, coming under the lordship of." It publicly acknowledges to whom the new recruit is committed.

While this may be the first time we see a clear statement of the triune nature and name of God, it certainly is not the last. This full statement about the person – God – we are making covenant with beautifully communicates the fullness of the relationship we are entering into. The New Testament idea of the triune nature of God is a picture of divine relationship, of divine community. There is perfect oneness in God, and it is that relationship we are being invited into. Participating in the life of Father, Son, and Holy Spirit has the power to transform every area of life, to remake our hearts, to re-energize our relationships – to make us disciples.

...teaching them to obey everything I have commanded you. Once someone has been initiated into the life of the Kingdom by establishing a clear, personal relationship with and commitment to Jesus – an intimate participation in the life and love of Father, Son, and Holy Spirit – then the lifelong task of teaching begins. The teaching

role of Jesus as "the Teacher" is a prominent theme in Matthew. A teacher held a very important place in ancient cultures (and in some Eastern cultures today). A teacher was responsible for delivering key discourses concerning truth and the right way to live. A teacher was to explain a matter so well that it became a part of a student's thinking and lifestyle. In Israel, a "Rabbi" was known for his unique teachings and for the disciples that followed his teaching and imitated his life. Jesus was acknowledged by all to be an important Rabbi in his day, and now he is charging his disciples to continue the role of teaching, to instruct and train a new generation of Jesus followers.

And what are they to teach these new disciples? Put simply, they are to teach the content of Messiah's instruction and they are to teach the resulting implications for their daily lives. This was the normal role of all Rabbis in Jesus' day. This had been the role of Jesus with his original disciples. Now this task was to be carried on by his followers in all nations.

I wonder at the way Jesus described the content of his teaching. He called it "everything I have commanded you." We tend to think of "commandments" as something we might read in the Old Testament. Why would Jesus be referring to his teaching as commandments? This word for "commanded" (Greek *entello*) always implies the authority of the one commanding; it involves a charge or a prescribed injunction. The teachings of Jesus were not just clever ideas or moral platitudes. The content of his instructions reflected the authority of the Kingdom of heaven. The words of Jesus were spirit and life, and they were to be embraced and lived out.

It's possible to teach something other than the things Jesus commanded. In that case, the content is not authoritative; it does not constitute a "commandment." It's also possible to faithfully teach what Jesus clearly commanded, his authoritative Messianic instructions. That's why some commentators actually refer to the five discourses in Matthew's gospel as "the Torah of the Messiah."

While teaching what Jesus has commanded, the task of disciple-making must also include "teaching them to obey." If the teaching is the authoritative word of the Lord, more than a respectful hearing is required. Those being taught are required to do more than go away and say, "Wasn't that a great word!" That word is to be obeyed!

The usual word for "obey" is not used by Jesus in this verse. Instead, we find the (Greek *tereo*) word for attending closely to, guarding, holding firmly to, consistently keeping. It actually involves more than simple obedience. It begins with an attitude of wanting to carefully hear and jealously guard whatever is being taught. It involves a zeal for the word that moves on to a commitment to observe and keep the word. It reflects a passionate love for and commitment to the Teacher and whatever the Teacher says, and not just an attempt to obey his instructions.

The teachings of Jesus are more than dogmatic doctrines, philosophical precepts, and propositional truths. The teachings of Jesus become relevant only to the extent that they are kept, are obeyed. The teachings of Jesus are to transform every area of the disciple's life – values, attitudes, relationships, words, and deeds – and to transform the new covenant Messianic community. The teachings of Jesus are commands that result in ethical obedience and personal transformation. Whether or not we are making disciples, are "teaching them to obey," will be shown by the transformation that takes place in their lives.

"Teaching them to obey" certainly includes teaching disciples about the need to obey. But practically speaking it also includes the need to show new disciples what obedience looks like. What does keeping the commands of Jesus imply in daily life? Instructing, modeling, training, mentoring, coaching – all in the context of a discipling relationship–are what is called for. We can't assume that everyone will automatically know how obedience to the instructions of Jesus translates into daily life. We have to teach them how to obey.

The final statement of Jesus provided a deep sense of assurance and confidence to those carrying on his mission. "And surely I am with you always, to the very end of the age." This statement could be literally translated, "And look, I myself will continue to be with you all the days, even to the consummation of the age." Jesus is not giving them a great commission and then cutting them loose. "Carry on my work, boys, and good luck!" They are joining him on his mission. They are becoming active participants in the mission of God on the earth. They will be representing the King, but they will also be enjoying the ongoing fellowship and partnership with the King in the process. He will be with them the whole of every day, every moment of every day, until the consummation of the age. In fact, Jesus will send his Holy Spirit to continue training, guiding, and empowering his followers.

These are words of comfort and encouragement. But they also cast a bright light on the importance of the mission. It will be Jesus who is continuing the mission of establishing the authority of the Kingdom of heaven on the earth – with and through his followers. They will not have the authority to redefine the mission but rather to simply be faithful to it in every generation. Making disciples...baptizing them...teaching them to obey.

The Command to *Learn* from Jesus

Dare I say that the call to disciple-making in the Great Commission looks very different from so many discipleship efforts we observe in the church today. We tend to trust a variety of pastoral and Christian education strategies —from Sunday school to small groups —to accomplish this task. But the mission Jesus left his followers seems to be much broader and to go much deeper than what we often experience. The life of a follower of Jesus, the way of discipleship, is a "yoked life."

The opportunity to attach ourselves to Jesus as his personal apprentices was given by Jesus to everyone equally. In Matthew chapter 11 Jesus stated, "all things have been committed to me by my Father" (verse 27). It sounds like his claim in the Great Commission. Everything, all authority, has been entrusted to King Jesus. Jesus then gives the great invitation: "Come to me, all..." (verse 28). Jesus is inviting all to become his disciples.

This passage begins with a prayer of Jesus, thanking the Father that the revelation of the Kingdom has actually been hidden "from the wise and learned" (verse 25), those who claimed to know all about God and God's purposes but were actually walking in darkness. Instead, the Father, through the instructions of Jesus, had revealed his Kingdom "to little children," to those who were considered small and of little account in the eyes of society. In fact, Jesus specifically invited those who are "weary and burdened" (verse 28). They are not the self-sufficient and the self-confident, but those who are weary as a result of hard labor and forced to carry heavy burdens. Later Jesus will condemn the Pharisees for putting heavy loads on the shoulders of the people (23:4). Jesus had come to offer them a different experience.

While everyone is invited to follow Jesus, he has no illusions about the fact that some will consider themselves too good, too important to stoop so low as to identify with this peasant Rabbi. Not everyone will be willing to humble themselves to be identified with Jesus, even though it is the greatest, the most significant of all possible callings.

In extending the invitation to follow him, Jesus uses a figure of speech familiar to all followers of the various Rabbis in first-century Israel. "**Take** my yoke upon you" (verse 29). While coming under a yoke is not the way we would ordinarily think about the life of a Jesus follower, for those original hearers, the figure of a "yoke" brought to mind specific ideas: (1) In general, it was connected to the wisdom of the Torah; (2) It described a personal relationship of loyalty and obedience; (3) It was a call to commit to a partnership in the mission of the Rabbi. The yoke was made up of the disciplines involved in a life of a true apprentice. The life of a disciple was a "yoked life."

Think of a picture of a wooden crosspiece that fastened over the necks of two animals and then attached to a plow. There was a task to be accomplished, namely plowing, but this task was to be accomplished by two oxen working in tandem. It implied a close personal relationship but also a working relationship between the two animals. It was common to yoke an older, stronger, more experienced animal to a younger, weaker, less experienced animal, in order to train (disciple) the young animal. The young one was participating in the task of plowing but only as a result of a clear, dependent partnership with the strong one.

And now you see a picture of the relationship between Jesus and his disciples. The call to discipleship is clear when we see that Jesus is commanding his followers to "**take**" his yoke and to "**learn**" from him. The word Jesus used for "learn" (Greek *manthano*) is related to a word we've already seen in the Commission in the command to "make disciples." Jesus is the great disciple-maker, calling us to the yoked life, a requirement that must be met by us before there is any chance of our discipling others.

Learning "from" Jesus is another way to describe the unique relationship between Master and student. The disciple didn't just go to class, take notes while listening to a lecture, and pass a test proving that he had been listening. The disciple was to master the content of the Rabbi's teaching, and also master the related lifestyle of the Rabbi. Learn from him, learn about him, learn to think like him, learn to live like him – learn him. The yoked life!

So, when a disciple "learns Jesus," what kind of Master will they learn? "For I am gentle and humble in heart." This One we are yoked to is gentle or meek, free from pretension, patient, longsuffering. He is the perfect example of one who is humbly submitted to the Father, who is willing to take the low position in relation to others, whose nature is to voluntarily give of himself to others. It's no wonder Jesus promised those who came under his yoke, "you will find rest for your souls."

I've often reflected on the importance of this idea of "rest" in Scripture. While a complete study would require another book, let me simply remind you of the "Sabbath Principle" of rest seen from the seventh day of creation to the various expressions of Sabbath in the Old Testament. The prophets summarized the state of blessedness for those who were fully submitted to God as "rest." On the other hand, the judgment of God was seen as an experience of "no rest." In the New Testament, Sabbath rest is promised to those who remain faithful to the Lord (Hebrews 4:3-11).

"For my yoke is easy and my burden is light" (verse 30). While coming under the yoke of Jesus, being fully devoted to learning him as his apprentice, certainly entails commitment and discipline, Jesus describes the experience of his yoke as "easy," as a yoke that is good, pleasant, kindly, easy to wear. The burden of the load being pulled under his yoke is "light," easy to bear. If the yoked experience was shared with any other partner, if the disciple was seeking to learn from any other master, it would surely be painful and grievous. But what greater joy could anyone experience than walking side-by-side with King Jesus, listening to his voice, observing his character, allowing his nature to bring transformation. Even during difficult days, walking under the yoke of Jesus would be pleasant indeed.

So how do we know if we are obeying the command to "learn" from Jesus? How do we know whether or not we are just going through the religious motions, making every effort to "work for" God? The promise of Jesus seems to be clear. We are experiencing "rest" in our souls as a result of our intimate connection with Jesus who is "gentle and humble in heart." What is called for is a heart-to-heart relationship with Jesus. The natural fruit of that relationship, of a life yoked with Jesus, will be rest, peace, harmony, wholeness, *Shalom*.

The Command to *Ask* for Workers

Jesus came as the King of the Kingdom and the Lord of the Harvest. He faithfully demonstrated the truth and power of God's reign on the earth in word and deed. And it must have seemed overwhelming at times. His coming inaugurated the rule of God, it brought the mission of God to a concrete time and place. At the same time, to carry the mission on to its consummation would require an army of disciple makers.

19

In chapter 9, Matthew records the ministry of Jesus as "going through all the towns and villages" (v. 35). Jesus was announcing the Good News of God's Reign everywhere he went, and Jesus was demonstrating the nature of God's Reign by "healing every disease and sickness." I can imagine that there was a lot of disease and sickness during Jesus' years of ministry. (Israel was not called Palestine until the second century, after Israel's second revolt against Rome, A.D. 132-135. After conquering Israel, Rome's emperor renamed the land of Israel Palastina (Palestine), after Philistia (Greek origin)) The heart of Jesus went out to all those he encountered. He saw them as "harassed and helpless," as "sheep without a shepherd." They were oppressed, downtrodden, wandering about without anyone to guide them. Jesus had certainly come as their Guide, but the work would need to be continued and expanded.

And so, Jesus gave his followers an important command. "**Ask** the Lord of the harvest, therefore, to send out workers into his harvest field" (9:38). Jesus saw that the "harvest is plentiful." The need and the opportunity to announce and extend God's rule was great. The potential to recruit and train followers and apprentices to Jesus was tremendous. At the same time, "the workers are few." Those actually working in the harvest field were few. The investment in the harvest was small. There was a clear and obvious need to ask the Lord of the harvest to send out workers.

It is up to the Lord to send workers out to participate in the Lord's harvest. It is not up to the followers of Jesus to initiate the sending. However, it is up to them to ask the Lord, to entreat the Lord, to even beg the Lord to send out workers. The first responsibility of the disciples, as is always the case, is to pray, to represent the need before God's throne, for workers – for committed, trained, empowered workers. It is the Lord who will then send them out, literally "cast them out" into the great harvest field of humanity in every generation.

It is also surely the responsibility of committed yoked disciples to be the first to volunteer. "Here am I Lord; send me." They will be the answer to their own prayers.

We are called to come under the yoke of Jesus, to learn him, to learn from him, be a committed, life-long apprentice of the Master. We are then commissioned to share in the mission of God, to make disciples in every culture, every place, for all time, until the end of days. We are commissioned to faithfully teach the instructions Jesus gave for life under God's rule. As we explore the commands of Jesus, our first goal is to learn to keep them, to live a life of joyful and loving obedience to the "Torah of the Messiah," and then to teach others to do the same. Let the adventure of the Yoked Life begin!

2 THE SERMON ON THE MOUNT (PART ONE)

I love the fact that Matthew organized the teachings of Jesus into five "Sermons." You can tell when each sermon ends because Matthew made the same closing statement each time, making note that "Jesus had finished" his teaching (7:28; 11:1; 13:53; 19:1; 26:1). Jesus taught the people, and especially his disciples, about the character of the reign he was bringing from heaven to earth.

The first sermon, the Sermon on the Mount, contains the core teachings of Jesus. In fact, some have called it the Constitution of the Community of Jesus. Taking the time to dive deeply into this Sermon should be approached with humility and excitement. There are a fairly large number of ways to interpret the Sermon on the Mount, from viewing it as ideals unattainable until the new heavens and the new earth, to ideals relevant only to saints. My approach will be to focus on the imperatives, the commands, found in the Sermon, and to take them seriously. If Jesus was giving authoritative instructions to his followers, and if he left us with the commission to teach others how to obey those commands, then accepting their authority in our lives is necessary. The Sermon on the Mount does so much more than paint a beautiful, utopian picture of life in "the sweet bye and bye." It describes the nature of the reign of God, inaugurated by Jesus at his first coming and to be consummated at his second coming, a description that instructs and challenges all committed followers of Jesus in the present day and every day.

It might be useful to point out that Jesus had a tremendous sense of humor. It was a more subtle, "Middle Eastern" humor, making use of irony and plays on words. He also made frequent use of hyperbole, a common form of communication used by the ancient Rabbis. It was simply a humorous exaggeration intended to move the audience to laugher and add graphic force to his words. It was a way to draw special attention to the point being made, hopefully making it easier to remember and discuss later. So, while we take the teaching of Jesus at face value, our understanding is also affected by our ability to put ourselves in his original audience.

Participation in the Kingdom

All of the teachings of Jesus were extensions of his original declaration, of the announcement of his Good News. "**Repent**, for the kingdom of heaven has come near" (4:17). It's interesting that this was also the pronouncement of John the Baptizer (3:2). It's not really possible to understand let alone participate in the meaning of the message without first responding to the invitation of Jesus.

This is the first command of Jesus, the one the other commands are built on. "Repent" is the first word of the Gospel. Unfortunately, it's not one of our favorite words. It brings to mind pictures of street preachers with a sandwich board announcing that "the end is near."

"Repent" gets at the core issue for us humans. Our problem is really that we are rebels, having chosen to live independently from our Creator. In fact, it is a choice we make many times every day. So, first of all, "repent" is a relational word, calling us to "turn" and to "return" back to a life of intimate relationship with God, a life with God at the center. So long as we continue to go our own way and do our own thing, wandering in the wilderness of our human commitment to independence, we will only know despair and death.

"Repent" also addresses the way we think. In the New Testament, "repent" (Greek *metanoeo*) literally means to have another mind, another attitude, another mental perspective. Even though we may think we are really smart, the simple fact is that living independently from God has made us stupid. Even our most clever educated guesses about life and the universe no doubt fall far short of the pure and beautiful truth found only in the mind of God. We have to learn to think differently. There is a desperate need for us to set aside our cleverness and learn to think God's thoughts.

That's why repentance assumes "confession," a word that means to agree with God. Whatever God's view might be on a matter, we assume that it is correct. When we are willing to agree with God's perspective, we are in a position to repent, to change our way of thinking and adopt God's way of thinking.

You see, the Gospel announcement of Jesus implied a radical new development. "The kingdom of heaven has come near." The reign of God had arrived. Because Jesus came as the King from heaven, his coming also brought the rule of God from heaven to earth. Jesus was not just a religious leader. Jesus was the official representative of the rule of God in heaven. Because Jesus was the King, the rule of God, the rule of heaven, came to earth with his arrival.

Submitting to the Rule of God now took on new meaning. King Jesus had come with the authoritative word of God. In fact, Jesus was the perfect, authoritative Living Word of God. From the moment of his coming the command was to listen and obey his teachings, his commands. Submission to God now meant submission to Jesus. And to do so would require deep repentance from the heart. Those following him needed to be ready to open their hearts and minds to receive his thoughts, his perspectives, and to adjust their thinking accordingly.

With that in mind, we are ready to step into the core teachings of Jesus. To be honest, I feel as though I need to take off my shoes as I consider the truths of the Sermon on the Mount. I am humbled and a bit fearful as I do so. But, trusting in the accuracy of the written revelation we have before us, and trusting in the Holy Spirit to guide and guard us, let's venture forth.

Characteristics of Participation in the Kingdom

The stage is set in 5:1. Jesus saw the crowds. While he had no illusions that they were all following him because they had repented at the good news, nevertheless he saw them as sheep without a shepherd, people who would need teaching and tending.

Jesus went "up on a mountainside." Some would see a parallel to Moses ascending Mt. Sinai at the giving of the Law and the covenant. While that may seem to stretch the analogy a bit, there is no question that Jesus was coming to them and teaching as a new Moses.

Jesus sat down to teach his disciples. It was the custom of Rabbis in those days to be seated with their students around them when they were about to present core teachings, the kind of teaching that was to be remembered, practiced and taught to others.

Jesus then began his Sermon with a series of eight blessings. Before diving into them it might be helpful to point out that the teachings of Jesus in the Sermon share some key thoughts with the prophet Isaiah, another prophetic voice from the house of David. Jesus was certainly teaching as a King and as a Law-giver or a priest, but he was also teaching as a prophet.

Think about the beautiful prophecy in Isaiah 61: "The Spirit of the Sovereign Lord is upon me, / because the Lord has anointed me to proclaim good news to the poor. / He has sent me to bind up the brokenhearted, / to proclaim freedom for the captives / and release from darkness for the prisoners, / to proclaim the year of the Lord's favor" (verses 1 & 2). Jesus chose this passage from Isaiah as his "mission statement" in his first sermon in the synagogue at Capernaum (Luke 4:18-19). It's no wonder those words echo in so much of his teaching.

Jesus began each of the pronouncements of blessing with a word (Greek *makarios*) that means fortunate or to be envied. It's almost like Jesus is saying, "Congratulations to...." And why are they so fortunate? Because the Kingdom of heaven has arrived. Because the King has come! That's why both the first and the last blessing or "beatitude" ends with the statement, "for theirs is the kingdom of heaven."

At the same time, the qualities that describe these fortunate ones reflect the fact that they have repented. They are the ones responding to the good news being brought to them by the King of God's Kingdom. As a result, they are ready to participate in the Messiah's rule.

And so, what do we learn about these new Kingdom participants?

1.   *The poor in spirit.* They are the poor Jesus was anointed to proclaim good news to. In fact, Luke's version of this statement (6:20) says, "Blessed are you who are poor." It doesn't do any good to discuss the difference between "poor in spirit" and "poor," since both carried the same meaning in the original context. The poor had come to symbolize those who were entirely dependent on God – because they had no choice. The "poor in spirit" are those who are entirely convinced of their need for God. They have abandoned any attempt to save themselves, to make themselves righteous. They are the ones who have repented. They are not self-sufficient, self-reliant or independent. They clearly see their need. As a result, they are Kingdom-ready.

2.   *Those who mourn.* Those who are grieving in the face of sin. They don't just agree that sin is a problem, calling for repentance. They have been stricken with the awful reality of the separation from God that has resulted from sin. They feel the

consequences of their rebellion against their Maker, and are filled with grief over the absence of God in their lives. For that reason, "they will be comforted." They will know God as their Comforter as a result of their heart-felt turning in repentance.

3.   *The meek.* The meek are the humble or the gentle and kind. They are the ones who have completely surrendered to God's rule and will in their lives. And it's not just a matter of religious ritual or a changed opinion. Their nature has been changed as a result of the extent of their humble submission as citizens of God's Kingdom. They are not the aggressors or the oppressors in any human relationship. While it would seem that the meek are those who could easily be victimized by the wicked, the promise of Jesus is, "they will inherit the earth." The words from Psalm 37:11 come to mind: "But the meek will inherit the land / and enjoy peace and prosperity." It is only those who have come under the authority of the King that will, in the end, inherit all the blessings the King has in store for them.

4.   *Those who hunger and thirst for righteousness.* "Righteousness" is one of the central ideas being taught by Jesus in the Sermon. Righteousness is simply right conduct in the eyes of God, in the context of God's covenant. Righteousness is both individual and corporate. Corporately, righteousness is justice. A truly repentant participant in the Messianic Kingdom will thirst for the way of life called for by the covenant, and for true justice in God's covenant community. As a result, "they will be filled." Their desire for true righteousness and justice will be fully satisfied under God's rule. While true justice may be found lacking outside of God's Kingdom, it will be fully realized under the reign of the King. However, this desire for righteousness is not just about "pie in the sky in the sweet bye and bye." Participants in the kingdom of heaven live each day, motivated by a desire to see righteousness and justice reign in and through their lives.

5.   *The merciful.* These repentant Kingdom participants are compassionate and generous. They are quick to forgive and provide aid to others. They are known for their covenant loyalty and commitment. They are committed to serving others, to being instruments of peace and deliverance – vessels of righteousness. Appropriately enough, "they will be shown mercy." They will know God's compassion and aid. Indeed, mercy is a very important characteristic of God. For that reason, Luke's account of some of the key teachings in the Sermon concludes with the statement, "Be merciful, just as your Father is merciful" (6:36), at the place where Matthew records, "Be perfect, therefore, as your heavenly Father is perfect" (5:48). The mercy of God and the mercy of God's people are core characteristics of the Kingdom.

6.   *The pure in heart.* Purity of heart refers to integrity, to a life of consistency

between the inner heart of a person and the outward life. Purity of heart is a heart and mind focused on God. It is a single-minded devotion to God, loving and serving God whole heartedly. Such a person "will see God." Seeing God summarizes the heart's desire of such a person. It is the person whose whole heart is focused on serving and pleasing God who will see God, who will perceive God in daily life and on into eternity. It's also true that those who were seeing Jesus were seeing God. They just didn't always recognize him. "Anyone who has seen me has seen the Father" (John 14:9).

7.   *The peacemakers.* The repentant participants in the Kingdom of heaven will always be on the side of peace. Specifically, they will promote and seek reconciliation in every situation. Where there are broken relationships, even where there are "enemies," the peacemaker will pursue peace, looking for a wise, effective strategy for bringing restoration. The commitment to reconciliation, to restoration, summarizes so many aspects of the character and purpose of God. It's no wonder that the peacemakers "will be called children of God." They reflect the character of their Father as God's reconciled, redeemed children.

8.   *Those who are persecuted because of righteousness.* "Righteousness" describes the nature of the rule of Christ, and it describes the character of those living under his rule. To be clear, to live out the righteousness of the Kingdom of heaven will result in followers of Jesus living contrary to the values of the surrounding culture. Those who are loyal to King Jesus above all others will find misunderstanding at best – if not opposition – from those whose loyalties lie elsewhere. The "kingdom of the world" wants people to choose sides, to declare their loyalty to one ideology or the other. To choose the side of King Jesus and not any position being promoted by the world will not be the path to popularity. "Theirs is the kingdom of heaven." Those who are willing to face opposition as a result of their commitment to the King are Kingdom-ready. They will know the favor of God in their lives.

To emphasize the last Beatitude, Jesus expanded on it. His followers, citizens of his Kingdom, will specifically experience insults and false accusations of evil. When they do, they should be congratulated. In fact, Jesus commanded them to "**Rejoice and be glad.**" They are not only to celebrate this situation, but they are also to be overjoyed! It almost sounds like they will have lost their minds. Who would ever experience joy for being falsely accused of being guilty of something they had never done?

First of all, it will be "because of me." The cause of this kind of persecution will not just be a matter of religious conviction or moral decision. It will be very personal.

It will be because of a specific case of loyalty to Jesus. And second, it will be because these Kingdom citizens are in the line of the old prophets. "In the same way they persecuted the prophets." The message of the prophets was rarely popular. In fact, it got some thrown into a pit and others executed. Speaking and living the message of the Kingdom can be very dangerous.

I find it interesting that Jesus announced his message with the command to **repent,** because his Kingdom had arrived. And then, after describing the characteristics of participation in that Kingdom, he commanded his followers to **rejoice.** Only those who have responded to the call to repentance and to full participation in the rule of Jesus will understand how it is possible to rejoice at opposition from those who have not repented, who are not loyal to his rule.

Children of Light

If opposition and persecution seem likely, I think it might be better to avoid being noticed. At least mix some of the values and agendas of the surrounding culture in so as not to be as obviously different. Can't I be a secret participant in the Kingdom?

Apparently not. Jesus followed up his description of the characteristics of Kingdom participants and the blessed promise of persecution with a command to be obvious, to stand out in the crowd, to influence the surrounding culture, even when it's not popular.

"You are the salt of the earth" (5:13). Most know that salt serves both to provide flavor and as a preservative. As salt, kingdom participants add a very important value to the world. They make a positive contribution just by being sprinkled on the world. It's interesting that the use of "salt" in both Mark 9:50 and Colossians 4:6 refers to the quality of relationships among the disciples. The example of covenant relationships will season the world and perhaps even preserve it from greater destruction.

"But if the salt loses its saltiness, how can it be made salty again?" You can't restore a salty flavor or a preservative quality after it is lost. To be effective, salt must be salty. Salt loses its saltiness when it becomes contaminated by being mixed with other chemicals. Salt also loses its saltiness if it becomes diluted. "It is no longer good for anything, except to be thrown out and trampled underfoot." In that day, salt that had lost its distinctiveness was scattered onto the soil of flat roofs to harden the soil – to make it easier for people to walk on. Followers of Jesus who have lost their saltiness are no longer able to contribute anything redemptive to society.

"You are the light of the world" (5:14). Light provided warmth and illumination. For that reason, the image of light was often used concerning truth, purity and God's presence. Jesus declared that he was "the light of the world" (John 8:12). Jesus was the Light sent from the Father into the darkness of the world, to light the way back to the Father. Now Jesus tells his followers that they too are to be light in the world.

"A town on a hill cannot be hidden." God's new Messianic Kingdom community is to serve as a town set on the top of a hill, where the lights shining from the community can be seen by all those needing light. They are not to be a town in a far-off hidden valley but a community that everyone can observe.

"Neither do people light a lamp and put it under a bowl." Can you imagine lighting a lamp or a candle only to hide it under some kind of bowl. Why light it in the first place? Lighting a lamp only has one purpose – to provide light in the room in which it is placed. "Instead they put it on its stand, and give light to everyone in the house." Not only is the lamp to be lit and placed where it can provide light, it is to be lifted up onto a lampstand so that everyone can see the light. This is a very public lamp, a very visible light.

"In the same way, **let your light shine** before others, that they may see your good deeds and glorify your Father in heaven." To make his point as clearly as possible, Jesus now gives an authoritative command. You must do everything you can to make the light that is in you through Jesus shine out so that others can see.

For you fans of Greek, this verb being used by Jesus is in the "aorist tense," which means that he is referring to specific cases of providing illumination. Jesus clarified his point by referring to people seeing "your good works." It is important for the watching world to see the difference being a repentant Christ-follower and Kingdom participant makes in the life of a human being. True repentance always results in observable life-change. While it's true that we are not saved by "works," it's also true that if salvation, if the grace of God and the influence of God's Spirit and Word do not produce relevant changes in thinking and behavior, it's safe to be concerned about our true heart response to God.

I love how Paul put it in his letter to the believers at Ephesus. "For you were once darkness, but now you are light in the Lord. Live as children of light" (5:8). Once we lived in darkness, in a lifestyle that reflected that darkness. Now we not only live in light, that light has found its way into our hearts. It only makes sense to expect that we will, as a result, live as children of light and no longer children of darkness.

Jesus also clarified the proper motivation for living as children of light. "That they may... Glorify your Father in heaven." Our goal is not for others to conclude that we are nice people, that we have cleaned our lives up, gotten our act together. It must always be very clear that any evidence of light–or of salty salt–is due only to God's reconciling work in our lives. It is the glory of God beginning to shine out in visible ways. We want people to see the light, but we want them to see that it is not a human light but a divine light. We want the glory of God to be clearly revealed in and through our lives, individually and corporately.

Examples of Participation in the Kingdom

While Jesus was teaching authoritatively as a "new Moses," it would be wrong to conclude that Jesus was bringing another Law to replace the old one taught by Moses. In fact, that charge was frequently brought against the disciples in the early church, even claiming that they were speaking "against the law" or teaching contrary to the Law (Acts 6:13; 18:13; 21:28). Not only was Jesus not teaching contrary to the Law, he was revealing the heart of the Law, the spirit of the Law. The traditional interpretation of the Law by the religionists of the day took a very superficial view of the Law and ended up missing the point. Jesus wants them to see the reality of what was in the heart of the Father when he revealed the Law. Jesus also taught from a prophetic perspective, in continuity with the message of the prophets.

To make that point clear, and before giving examples of his approach to the Law, Jesus said, "Do not think that I have come to abolish the Law or the Prophets" (5:17). Jesus did not come to separate himself or to throw away the revelation of God in the Law and Prophets. Instead, Jesus came "to fulfill them." Jesus himself was the fulfillment of everything revealed in the Law and the Prophets. His teaching revealed the heart and meaning of the Law and Prophets. His message and ministry were the culmination of the Law and Prophets. In fact, it was the religious traditions being taught in his day that served to abolish the Law and Prophets.

Jesus emphasized this point even more graphically by pointing out that "not the smallest letter, not the least stroke of a pen" in the Law and Prophets would disappear. Verse 18 is actually the first time we see the words, "Truly I tell you" at the beginning of a statement. It was the way Jesus emphasized the importance of what he was about to say. "Pay careful attention to the following words." Even the smallest detail of the Law was inspired by God and was to be considered authoritative in people's lives. Everything revealed in the Law and the Prophets would remain in force until every detail had come to pass at the end of all things.

Jesus condemned those who set aside the true meaning of God's revelation to be replaced by their teaching. On the other hand, Jesus blessed those who practice and teach the right principles revealed in the Law and the Prophets. A superficial, religious understanding of God's revelation may have resulted in a certain kind of righteousness, but it was an external, religious righteousness. Jesus was calling for a higher, deeper kind of righteousness that could only come by exploring and embracing the true meaning of the Law and Prophets. In fact, those who did not embrace this greater righteousness "will certainly not enter the kingdom of heaven."

ᵔᵕᵔ

The teaching of Jesus did not set aside the Law, rather, it explained the heart of the matter, making a heart connection possible for the hearers. Understanding the approach of Jesus, the call for Kingdom righteousness, would make possible a heart-to-heart relationship with the Father and the experience of genuine heart change. The examples of participation in the Messianic Kingdom assume the presence of the characteristics of Kingdom participants. In fact, Jesus teaches the Law and the Prophets with those characteristics in mind.

Jesus provided five powerful examples of the true fulfillment of the Law in the lives of his followers.

The Example of Reconciliation

Jesus began by stating a well-known commandment from the Law. "You shall not murder, and anyone who murders will be subject to judgment" (5:21). The first half is the sixth commandment in Exodus 20:13. The word for "murder" in both the sixth commandment and in this verse refers to an intentional and unlawful taking of another life. It is "first degree murder." The second half of the statement of Jesus, "anyone who murders will be subject to judgment" is not found in the sixth commandment. It seems to be added to focus on the ultimate consequence of murder. The traditional focus by the religious teachers of the day was on the need for judgment on those who commit an intentional, premeditated murder.

The heart of the matter, the essence of the sin involved, is then described by Jesus. The traditional focus was introduced with, "You have heard that it was said." Jesus now switched gears by saying, "But I tell you." It sounds like Jesus is going to contradict the sixth commandment and replace it with a new commandment. Instead, Jesus is going to go beyond a superficial focus on the most extreme case of murder to get to the real heart of the matter. What is the real issue from God's perspective?

"Anyone who is angry with a brother or sister will be subject to judgment." It goes beyond a case of intentional murder. The real problem from God's vantage point is a certain kind of anger in the human heart. It is that kind of anger that will make someone subject to judgment.

Jesus provided two examples of the consequences of anger, no doubt drawing on the use of Rabbinic hyperbole. Any who calls someone "Raca" could be answerable to a court. Calling someone "Raca" would be like us telling a person they were useless, a waste of skin. If you call someone a "Fool," you are in danger of going to hell. In the Old Testament wisdom writings, a fool was someone who was intentionally immoral, the result of living with the absence of the fear of the Lord. Frankly, Jesus did not hesitate to refer to someone as a "fool" in his parables (Luke 12:20). His examples simply draw attention to the fact that the real issue is anger, the kind of anger that might actually wish that someone did not exist or behave as if they did not exist, and that this kind of anger would have consequences.

Jesus then got to the heart of his teaching with a series of commands. They were not only suggestions in light of what he had just said, they were the punch line, the authoritative word in the light of his teaching, commands to be embraced and obeyed.

The commands of Jesus in this passage go even beyond the problem of anger and treating others hatefully. Jesus clarified by painting a picture of a believer at worship. "If you are offering your gift at the altar and there remember that your brother or sister has something against you." This is a case of someone who has a complaint, a claim against this worshipper, resulting in a broken relationship. The root may or may not be anger, but in any case, a relational division has occurred as a result of the interaction between two people.

"**Leave** your gift there in front of the altar. First **go** and **be reconciled** to them, then come and **offer** your gift" (5:24). This series of four commands give a clear sense of the Kingdom expectation in the case of a broken or injured relationship. The central command is, "**Be reconciled**." Do whatever it takes to mend and restore the relationship. And don't hesitate to do so. "**Leave**" your sacrifice and "**go**" immediately. From God's perspective, restoring a broken relationship is more important than a religious exercise. In fact, the character of God will be revealed in the restoring of a relationship.

Jesus then emphasized the importance and urgency of seeking reconciliation. "**Settle matters** quickly with your adversary" could be literally translated, "Become friends with your enemy." Don't wait until a difference escalates and you end up in court. Don't wait for the court to settle matters. Take the initiative to settle the matter and to restore friendship with someone who has become your adversary.

So, it's not just a matter of avoiding selfish anger, let alone not murdering someone. A Kingdom participant will place such a high value on relationships that any injuring or breaking of a relationship will be considered unacceptable. And it will be so unacceptable, the need for reconciliation will be considered so urgent, everything else will be put on hold until that relationship has been healed. That is the heart of the matter for Jesus. That is a "greater righteousness," and Jesus expects his followers to live it out consistently.

The Example of Relational Faithfulness

Once again Jesus began by stating the tradition from the Law, in this case, the seventh commandment. "You shall not commit adultery" (5:27). "Adultery" in both the Old and New Testaments refers to covenant unfaithfulness, to the breaking of a covenant. It's possible to have a very superficial, rigid, legalistic view of what constitutes adultery and covenant unfaithfulness.

Just a note about legalism: "Legalism" is a focus on the "letter of the law," narrowing the meaning of the Law as far as possible by having a view of the external aspects only. In the end, legalism is not designed to enforce a very rigorous application of the Law as much as it is a search for loopholes. Legalism is also a control issue, a way to (attempt) to control the details of one's life, including one's life with God, as well as an attempt to control the personal lives of others. Frankly, Jesus will have none of it, but will rather explore the heart of the matter, the heart of God as revealed in a commandment.

"But I tell you that anyone who looks at a woman lustfully has already committed adultery with her in his heart" (5:28). The heart of the matter is an issue of desire and intent. Looking "lustfully" describes looking at a woman with a desire to have sex with her. It's not just the act of adultery but the desire that could lead to adultery that Jesus has in mind. Unfaithfulness begins in the heart, in the mind, and in the desires.

It's obvious that a woman could look lustfully at a man. However, in Jesus' day, women were not viewed as having the same rights as men. In fact, a woman caught in adultery would be executed. And so, the issue is addressed primarily to men.

Jesus then stated a series of commands. The fact that this is another example of Rabbinic hyperbole served to emphasize the importance of what Jesus was saying. "If you right eye causes you to stumble, **gouge** it out and **throw** it away" (5:29). It would be impossible to look at someone lustfully without looking with the eyes. So, Jesus was clear that in this case, it is the eye that causes someone to stumble. It is the wrong focus of the eye, matched to a wrong desire in the heart, that creates a stumbling block. To emphasize the danger of unfaithfulness, Jesus essentially said that it would be better to be blind. The consequences of adultery are too severe to ignore the process of adultery. "It is better for you to lose one part of your body than for your whole body to be thrown into hell." Jesus is not so much saying that someone who looks lustfully at another person will go to hell so much as he is saying that covenant unfaithfulness is extremely dangerous.

Jesus then added another command to expand on this point. "And if your right hand causes you to stumble, **cut** it off and **throw** it away" (5:30). It's not just sight but also touch that can contribute to adultery. It would be better to lose the ability to touch than to misuse it in a way that reflects the desires of the heart. Once again, Jesus emphasized the severity of the matter. "It is better for you to lose one part of your body than for you whole body to go into hell."

Wrong desires take place in the heart and the mind. It's possible for a blind man and someone with no right hand to have a desire that sets him up for some form of unfaithfulness. However, the teaching of Jesus is very clear and practical, emphasizing the process and the consequences of unfaithfulness.

The issue of adultery easily leads to a discussion of divorce. "Divorce" is the official breaking of a covenant relationship. Divorce was very common in Jesus' day, but only men were allowed to divorce their spouse. A husband could divorce his wife for almost any reason. He could divorce her if she "spoiled a dish," or even if she no longer found favor in the eyes of her husband. If a man found a young woman who he considered "fairer" than his wife, it could be ruled as his wife falling out of favor and as   grounds for divorce.

Clearly, the view of Jesus about relational faithfulness would not allow for that practice of divorce. It's no wonder that Jesus followed up his teaching about adultery with a brief statement about divorce. "It has been said, 'Anyone who divorces his wife must give her a certificate of divorce'" (5:31). While a Jewish man could divorce his wife for any reason, proper religious and legal procedures had to be followed. It was important to look pious while sending your wife away. "But I tell you that anyone who divorces his wife, except for sexual immorality, makes her the victim of adultery, and anyone who marries a divorced woman commits adultery" (5:32). Jesus connected the issue of adultery with that of divorce, of covenant unfaithfulness leading to covenant breaking. While the Rabbis maybe supported a very skewed view of divorce, it did not represent God's view. From heaven's perspective, there was only one way to break a marriage covenant, and that was with sexual immorality.

The irony is clear. If a woman was caught having sex with a man outside of marriage, she would normally be stoned. For Jesus to allow this as the only legitimate case for divorce, covenant unfaithfulness leading to covenant breaking, expressed his complete lack of support for how his society viewed the rights of men over their wives. When a man and a woman pledged themselves to each other, entering into a covenant relationship "before God and these witnesses," that covenant relationship was viewed by God as sacred and inviolable. A wife who was sent away by her husband for any reason and who was then married by another man made that man into adulterer. The reason was simple: God considered that wife to still be married to the first man. No matter how the covenant breaking was rationalized by the man, God did not view it that way.

So, the teaching of Jesus about divorce was simply an extension of his emphasis on the need to guard the sacredness of relational faithfulness. When a man was looking for a reason to divorce his wife, he was already committing adultery, he was already unfaithful, in his heart.

The Example of Integrity

Jesus then addressed the issue of oath taking. "Again, you have heard that it was said to the people long ago, 'Do not break your oath, but fulfill to the Lord the vows you have made'" (5:33). This traditional statement is not a specific quote from any passage in the Law. However, the overall sense of the Law would certainly lead to this understanding (cf. Leviticus 5:4; Numbers 5:19; 30:2). The third commandment about not misusing or misrepresenting the Lord's name is also in the background.

Of particular relevance is the statement in Deuteronomy 6:13: "Fear the Lord your God, serve him only and take your oaths in his name," and also Deuteronomy 10:20: "Fear the Lord your God and serve him. Hold fast to him and take your oaths in his name." Taking an oath in the Lord's name was considered especially sacred and not to be broken for any cause. For that reason, the Rabbis looked for lesser things to take an oath by, resulting in potential loopholes. They engaged in endless debates about levels of oath taking, but Jesus considered the debate to be missing the point.

"But I tell you, do not swear an oath at all" (5:34). Jesus then rehearsed the various levels of oath taking, telling them to avoid every one of them. "...either by heaven, for it is God's throne; or by the earth, for it is his footstool; or by Jerusalem, for it is the city of the Great King." It was absurd to think that various levels of oath taking could be defined in order to avoid taking an oath in the Lord's name, since everything came from the Lord and belonged to the Lord. "And do not swear by your head, for you cannot make even one hair white or black." While this statement was made before the advent of hair coloring, it further illustrates that the religious, legalistic approach to oath taking was an attempt, not only to find loop holes in the oath but also to be in control in the process.

Jesus then gave a very clear, authoritative command. "All you need to say **is** simply 'Yes' or 'No'" (5:37). Jesus expects his followers to be honest in everything they say. He expects them to live a life of simple and consistent integrity. When they say, "Yes," they need to really mean it. And if they say, "No," they need to mean what they say. In fact, anyone who is consistently honest does not need to take an oath.

"...anything beyond this comes from the evil one." As Jesus would later say, the devil is a liar and the father of lies. Any desire to get around the need to speak an honest "Yes" or "No" is at the heart of lying, and therefore reflects the nature of the devil. A true representative of the Messianic Kingdom will always speak the simple

---

truth, with no ulterior motives, no hidden agenda, no prevarication. Just be honest!

The Example of Peacemaking

Jesus had previously declared, "Congratulations to the peacemakers." But peacemaking can be a difficult idea. What was needed were specific, concrete examples.

"You have heard that it was said, 'Eye for eye, and tooth for tooth'" (5:38). When this law was first set forth by God through Moses (Exodus 21:24; Leviticus 24:20; Deuteronomy 19:21) it was actually quite revolutionary. Ancient law codes prescribed different levels of punishment for different classes of people. The poor endured a much greater punishment for the same crime as the rich. This law, also called the *lex talionis* (law of retaliation) stated that in every case and for every person, the punishment must match the crime. It was certainly a fair, just law. And Jesus was certainly not suggesting that it be set aside.

However, in practice this way of establishing justice in a society tended to result in a cycle of violence. If you poke my eye out, I have the right if not the obligation to poke yours out! It called for an attitude of retribution, doing whatever it took to balance the moral scales. The outcome of the Law worked against the spirit and character of the Kingdom of heaven.

In the light of that, Jesus gave four authoritative commands to his followers, each one illustrating a "greater righteousness."

"But I tell you, do not resist an evil person." Don't set yourself against him. Don't oppose or withstand him. Don't feel like you have to stand your ground and defend your rights in the face of an evil person. Don't set yourself up as the judge and jury, let alone executioner, if you are wronged by another. This is the principle idea that Jesus was illustrating. Somehow a citizen of God's Kingdom must allow God to be the Judge, to leave retribution and even vengeance in God's hands. So, what might that look like?

"If anyone slaps you on the right cheek, **turn** to them the other cheek as well." When someone wished to publicly offend, humiliate or challenge another, they backhanded that person with their right hand, slapping on the right cheek. I don't know about you, but I think I would have a hard time responding peacefully to a public slap. However, if I wanted to pursue peace and reconciliation in every situation, I would need to obey the command of Jesus in this case.

"And if anyone wants to sue you and take your shirt, **hand over** your coat as well." The Law of Moses was compassionate in the case of an unpaid debt. A neighbor's cloak was to be returned by sunset, "because that cloak is the only covering your neighbor has" (Exodus 22:26–27). So, Jesus was referring to someone who was violating that law, demanding that a person's shirt be handed over permanently. It is a clear case of injustice and oppression. But rather than resist that injustice, find a way to fight back, or just refuse to hand the coat over, Jesus advised that the coat be handed over along with the shirt. Someone committed to making peace, to pursuing reconciliation, will not be willing to fight over their right to their shirt, or any item of clothing. Peace is more valuable, more important. Peace is the goal.

"If anyone forces you to go one mile, **go** with them two miles." In the Roman Empire, soldiers had the right to conscript someone to carry their gear for one mile. Even having to submit to the Empire was a grievous injustice for the Jewish people. A Roman soldier demanding that a Jew carry the weapons of injustice for a mile just rubbed salt into a person's wounds. Can you imagine what a soldier might think if a person, having finished the required mile, turned and said, "May I carry your gear a second mile?" How might that affect the thinking of the soldier? Would it contribute to the goal of peacemaking? Might it eventually end the cycle of violence?

"**Give** to the one who asks you, and do not turn away from the one who wants to borrow from you." A peacemaker is a nonviolent lover of reconciliation, and a peacemaker is also generous. It's only normal to insist on terms of repayment when loaning something to someone. It's common to wonder whether or not someone will ever repay us, or to wonder whether they will make a wise use of what we give them. Someone pursuing peace will just give, demanding nothing in return.

The example of peacemaking is perhaps the most difficult of the teachings of Jesus about participation in his Kingdom, and for that reason, it has tended to be the most controversial. But, surely it's not difficult to see that someone with a heart for peace, someone with a passion for reconciliation, will be willing to set aside personal grievances and the need for retribution. If, in fact, some form of retribution is needed, perhaps it's best to leave vengeance in the hands of God. We can trust God to always rule and act in a perfectly just manner. Our call is to a life governed by love.

The Example of Perfect Love

It seems as though Jesus has been leading step by step into a full description of the greater righteousness that will be the hallmark of his rule. He started by describing the characteristics of truly repentant, fully participating citizens of his Messianic Kingdom, pronouncing a blessing on what could have seemed like odd qualities. God's favor would rest on the "poor in spirit," "those who mourn," "the meek," "those who hunger and thirst for righteousness." "The merciful," "the pure in heart," "the peacemakers," and "those who are persecuted because of righteousness" were to be congratulated. They were to "rejoice and be glad," finding themselves at the heart of God's Kingdom and the heart of God.

After clarifying the need for these Kingdom characters to have influence in the world, Jesus confirmed that he was not replacing the Law and the Prophets but providing a deeper insight into the interior spirit of the Law. The ones experiencing heart transformation as a result of their participation in the Kingdom of heaven would experience the writing of the Law on their hearts, as Ezekiel had prophesied. They would not be satisfied with only refusing to murder someone, they would be liberated from a heart of hatred and anger, demonstrating a commitment to reconciliation. Just following the religious rules about adultery and divorce would not be enough, but they would show an ability to maintain faithfulness in their hearts toward their spouses, and even in all the covenant relationships God provided them. They would not be willing to play games with religious oaths but would live a life of honesty and integrity. While fair punishment and retribution is a good thing, these Kingdom citizens would place peace as a higher value.

And now, Jesus brings us to the bottom line. "You have heard it was said, 'Love your neighbor and hate your enemy'" (5:43). It is true that Leviticus 19:18 called for a love for one's neighbor. In fact, in Leviticus the Lord also commanded the people to love their neighbor "as yourself," placing a very high and personal priority on love of neighbor. Jesus included this commandment when he summarized the "great commandment," placing it second only to loving "the Lord your God with all your heart and with all your soul and with all your mind," declaring that "all the Law and the Prophets hang on these two commandments" (Matthew 22:36-40).

But, the religious leaders of the day tried to get around the commandment to love one's neighbor by asking the question, "Who is my neighbor" (Luke 10:29). Another classical example of superficial, legalistic thinking. It's interesting that Jesus answered that question with the Parable of the Good Samaritan, concluding with a question of his own, "Which of these three do you think was a neighbor to the man who fell into the hands of robbers?" He made it clear that showing mercy was the essential quality of neighborliness.

However, there is no statement in the Law commanding people to "hate your enemy." In fact, the Old Testament Law gives instructions about the need to return an ox or donkey that had wandered off, even if it belonged to an enemy (Exodus 23:4). The statement to "hate your enemy" or to "hate the children of darkness" was found in the writings at Qumran, those we call the Dead Sea Scrolls. That sentiment did not just reflect a fringe religious group but rather represented the common Jewish contempt for all non-Jews – Gentiles. This religious exclusion of everyone who was "other," based on a profound self-righteousness and willingness to hate and reject a whole class of people, was utterly out of place in the rule King Jesus was bringing.

In fact, Jesus followed up with two authoritative commands. "But I tell you, **love** your enemies and **pray** for those who persecute you" (5:44). Every human being – not just those in the "in crowd" – is to be loved unconditionally by followers of King Jesus. Not only are they to love, they are also to represent them before the Father in prayer, beseeching God for mercy and blessing.

"...that you may be children of your Father in heaven." Above all else, God *is* love. God's love is not conditional and exclusive to a select, acceptable few. God's love is personal, voluntary, unconditional, and unlimited. Sharing in the heart of God, reflecting the glory of God, will be shown by the quality of one's love for others. In fact, it could be said that the true measure of this "greater righteousness" is the way a Kingdom citizen treats other people.

"He causes his sun to rise on the evil and the good, and sends rain on the righteous and the unrighteous." The Father blesses and provides for everyone equally. It's not possible to earn God's favor. He freely provides grace through the work of his Son. The Father's love is continually seeking expressions of self-giving, looking for opportunities to bless others.

"If you love those who love you, what reward will you get? Are not even the tax collectors doing that? And if you greet only your own people, what are you doing more than others? Do not even pagans do that?" Anything less than unconditional, self-giving love is no better than what is normally shown by the hated tax collectors and Gentiles. Using a religious rationale is no excuse. The Father of our Lord Jesus Christ and the King of his heavenly Kingdom, calls his people to love in the same way that God loves (Sentence doesn't make sense. Not sure what you're saying—too many pronouns.).

༓

"**Be perfect**, therefore, as your heavenly Father is perfect." Perfect love is simply the kind of love God has freely given. Jesus is not suggesting that his followers reflect all of the perfections of the Father's nature and attributes, but rather that they love like the Father loves. In the end, that will be the clearest sign of their participation under his rule. In the end...

"Love is patient, love is kind.
"It does not envy, it does not boast, it is not proud.
"It does not dishonor others, it is not self-seeking, it is not easily angered, it keeps no record of wrongs.
"Love does not delight in evil but rejoices with the truth.
"It always protects, always trusts, always hopes, always perseveres.
"Love never fails" (1 Corinthians 13:4-8).

And that is a true description of a citizen of the Messianic Kingdom!

3 THE SERMON ON THE MOUNT (PART TWO)

The Sermon on the Mount always feels like "holy ground" to me. I almost hesitate to do anything more than humbly and prayerfully listen to the voice of the Lord revealing the core of his teaching to us. The Sermon paints a beautiful picture of the unique nature of the King and his Kingdom. It describes the quality of his rule and of those who come under his rule in simple but profound statements.

In Matthew 5 Jesus authoritatively proclaimed the truth about what had been revealed in the Law and the Prophets, in the Old Testament. In the process, we are able to explore in greater depth the heart of God and the nature of Kingdom righteousness. The life of a sincerely repentant participant in the Kingdom of heaven is described, a life governed by King Jesus and by the Law of Love.

In chapter 6, Jesus carefully unfolded the kind of personal relationship with God he had in mind for his followers. What does that relationship look like, and how does it contrast to other religious attempts to "know God."

Chapter 7 brings a glorious summation of the "greater righteousness" that marks the rule of God, the way that kind of righteousness affects relationships with God and with others. The Sermon ends with several ways to present the final need to submit to the authoritative rule and teachings of the King. Jesus is not just providing inspirational, devotional thoughts for Christians but precepts and commands to be obeyed. Whether or not they are obeyed will have lasting consequences for his listeners.

I'm amazed at the fact that Jesus never critiqued the Roman Empire or even the regional rule of the Herodian family. Jesus' issue was with the religious leaders of his generation. Jesus was passionately concerned about how religious leaders understand God, how they interpret the Word of God, and how they live out the message in their lives and relationships. Jesus was even convinced that their religious thinking would have a toxic effect on the lives of those who follow them.

Listening to the words of Jesus in the Sermon requires us to examine our own religious ideas and practices. Perhaps doing so will lead us to a new experience of repentance and a new submission to the righteous rule of King Jesus.

A Deeper Relationship with the Father

Almsgiving, prayer, and fasting are the three most common elements of any world religion, and they were commonly practiced by Jewish leaders and people in Jesus' day. It's not the practice of these kinds of things that Jesus objects to, but rather the motivation for practicing them.

The general principle was stated right at the beginning. "**Be careful** not to practice your righteousness in front of others to be seen by them" (6:1). Be aware of why you are engaging in certain religious practices. Be on the alert for the possibility of doing them in order to impress others with your spirituality. "If you do, you will have no reward from your Father in heaven." If your desire is to impress others, doing so will be your only reward. However, if your spiritual practices are done before God in the context of your sincere, authentic heart relationship with God, then you will gain the kind of results only God can give.

Almsgiving. "So when you give to the needy" (6:2). There was no question about a follower of Jesus showing mercy and generosity toward those who didn't have enough. With over 2,000 relevant passages of Scripture, a person's attitude toward and care of the poor is a very high priority to God. It was assumed that those practicing a "greater righteousness" would be generous with the poor. The religious people of the day certainly were, but they had ulterior, self-centered motives. Jesus once again used Rabbinic hyperbole to draw attention to his point and illicit a response from his hearers. "Do not announce it with trumpets," painting a picture of almsgivers marching through the streets with a brass band leading the way. Although that never happened, it graphically makes the point. "...to be honored by others," the real motivation of these generous givers. In the end, they wanted to be noticed as being generous, they wanted to be honored in the process, and so did whatever needed to be done in order to accomplish that goal.

"...as the hypocrites do." The role of a "hypocrite" in ancient society seems to sum up what is wrong with this picture. A "hypocrite" was an actor in a play. Ancient plays allowed actors to play several roles by wearing a variety of masks. A hypocrite was a play-actor, a mask-wearer, a performer, a poser, a faker. While that may have been acceptable in the theater, it was not in a religious context. However, it was also common in religious contexts. "I tell you, they have received their reward in full." Any benefit a hypocritical almsgiver was hoping to receive would be limited to the complements they received from those looking on.

"But when you give to the needy, do not let your left hand **know** what your right hand is doing" (6:3). The use of the hyperbole was still present, since a human hand doesn't know anything about what the other is doing. However, the image communicates the desirability for self-forgetfulness when being generous toward the poor. Indeed, all acts of service are to be essentially selfless, done as much as possible in a place of hiddenness, "so that your giving may be in secret." In that way, they will receive a blessing from the Father, "who sees what is done in secret." Their reward will come in the context of their personal relationship with the Father, who doesn't need a trumpet to draw attention to generosity when it comes from the heart. This kind of giving will be pleasing to the Father, since mercy and generosity are at the core of the Father's heart.

Prayer. Communication with the Father heart-to-heart is central to a personal relationship with the Father. Unfortunately, it is possible to pray hypocritically. "They love to pray standing in the synagogues and on the street corners to be seen by others" (6:5). Jesus was not criticizing public prayer but rather praying in public in such a way that was designed to draw attention to the piety of the one praying. As with hypocritical almsgiving, "they have received their reward in full." Instead, the one communicating with the Father should do so in a way that reflects the intimacy of the moment. "But when you pray, **go** into your room, close the door and **pray** to your Father, who is unseen" (6:6). Jesus not only expected his Kingdom representatives to pray, he commanded them to pray, but pray to their Father who sees their hearts. The "room" being referred to by Jesus is an inner closet or storage room, a place that is normally unused, a place of intimacy with the Father. "Then your Father, who sees what is done in secret, will reward you."

Jesus then commented on pagan approaches to prayer. "Do not keep on babbling like pagans" (6:7). Pagan religions practiced a variety of prayer formulas, from a repetition of unintelligible words that were supposed to have magical powers to prayers that repeated the names of the gods over and over again. "They think they will be heard because of their many words." Pagan religion seeks to find ways to manipulate the gods with the right combination of words, in a desire to get the gods to bless or curse. A personal relationship was never in view. "Do not be like them." Jesus was not criticizing the use of written prayers repeated at certain times. If he had done so he would have ended up condemning the use of the Psalms in prayer and worship, a practice common in both Judaism and Christianity. Instead, Jesus was commenting on a manipulative, "babbling" as some sort of prayer expression.

Prayer is not talking God into your agenda, "for your Father knows what you need before you ask him." Prayer is communication with God in the context of a personal relationship with God. It is the essence of that relationship.

Jesus then provided a wonderful model prayer. In Luke's account, this prayer follows the request from the disciples, "Lord, teach us to pray" (11:1). "Teach us to pray" is perhaps one of the first prayer requests we should learn. Jesus was not just suggesting a possible prayer. He was providing authoritative instructions about prayer. "**Pray** then in this way" (6:9). "Pray" is not just a commandment, it is given in the present continuous tense, commanding a certain lifestyle of prayer. This beautiful prayer not only teaches us our priorities when we pray, it also teaches us the priorities of our faith walk. It has six requests, the first three concerning the intention toward God on the part of the one praying, and the last three pertaining to their daily lives. All six are also expressed as imperative expressions, not given as a command but rather an indication of the need to pray confidently. Let me quote it in the old King James Version.

Our Father which art in heaven. Because of the work of Jesus and the salvation he brought, all believers can count God as their Father, a privilege not known before.

*...**hallowed** be thy name.* "May your name be **revered**," be accounted as holy. Kingdom worshipers seek to honor God as holy at all times, and they are careful to not take the name of the Lord in vain, or to misuse the name of the Lord. Their attitude toward God's name is demonstrated by their life of loyalty and faithfulness to the Lord.

*Thy Kingdom **come**.* "May your kingdom **come**." The entire background and focus of the teaching and ministry of Jesus was based on his core message. "The kingdom of heaven is at hand." Because Jesus was the King who had come, the rule of heaven had come to earth, to be established among human beings. Praying for the increasing rule of God will always be a high priority for the King's loyal subjects.

*Thy will be **done**.* "May your will be **done**." May the eternal purpose and good pleasure of the Lord be accomplished in and through the lives of his children. *...in earth, as it is in heaven.* This added statement can apply to both the request for the Kingdom to come and for God's will to be done. God rules in heaven. God's throne is in heaven. But God's long-term desire is for that rule to extend to the earth, among human beings. Heaven rules, and Jesus brought that authority to earth. The request is not for earth to rule but for human beings to embrace and submit to heaven's rule, bringing the blessedness of that rule into their daily human experience.

Give us this day our daily bread. "Daily bread" is a word used only here in the New Testament. It is bread enough for today. A working man would go out to labor early in the morning with the hopes of bringing home enough income to provide for the needs of his family for the next day. It brings to mind the instructions about manna God gave to the Israelites in the wilderness. "The people shall go out and gather a day's portion every day" (Exodus 16:4). God provided only enough for each day, every day. "Daily bread" is God's promise. While it may seem like a lack of planning, it is a great way to facilitate our daily intimate dependence on God. "...that I may test them, whether or not they will walk in my instruction."

And forgive us our debts as we forgive our debtors. Most of our English translations render "debts" as "trespasses" or "sins." It is certainly true that the debt we owe God is due to our insistence on going our own way, our rebellion against God. And that is the essence of sin. Jesus added the phrase, "as we forgive those who owe us a debt," The connection between the flow of forgiveness from God to us and from us to others is so important Jesus will return to that theme in verses 14 and 15.

And lead us not into temptation, but deliver us from evil. This is perhaps the most confusing request of the prayer. The focus is on the need to be rescued or delivered from evil, or literally, "from the evil one." Jesus had experienced forty days of temptation at the hands of the evil one and was familiar with the need to be kept safe during times when the devil is attempting to bring discouragement or defeat into our lives. The reference to "temptation" is not about the training "tests" God occasionally provides us but rather enticing trials engineered by our enemy designed to trick and trip us. We know, and can confidently pray, that God will not only keep us safe but will bring us out of the temptation in a way that demonstrates the authority of Jesus and his ultimate defeat of Satan.

Most of the early manuscripts do not include the final doxology. However, a document as early as *The Didache*, or *The Teaching of the Twelve Apostles*, an early catechism from the late first century, includes the doxology. It certainly indicates that the "Lord's Prayer" or the "Our Father" was already a regular part of the worship practice of the early church and included a final expression of praise. *For thine is the kingdom, and the power, and the glory, for ever. Amen.*

Since mercy, self-giving love, forgiveness and restoration are central to the heart and character of God, and since prayer is all about relationship with God, it's no wonder that Jesus reemphasized the need for reciprocal forgiveness. Thinking that we can receive God's forgiveness and then refuse to extend that to others shows a distinct lack of understanding of both God's nature and the nature of relationship with God. Positively, "If you forgive others for their transgressions, your heavenly Father will also forgive you" (6:14). The dynamic of God's loving, merciful forgiveness is like a river that flows from God's throne. Our commitment to being a source as well as a receiver of that river is vital. Negatively, "If you do not forgive others, then your father will not forgive your transgressions" (6:15). If the flow of forgiveness is stopped up in our own stubborn refusal to forgive others, we cannot expect it to continue to flow into our lives. (It's interesting that Jesus does not use the word for "debts" here but the one for "transgressions.)

Fasting. "Whenever you fast" (6:16). Fasting as a discipline of abstinence is another common element of religion, usually abstinence from food. However, you may view fasting, one simple thing seems to be clear from Scripture; fasting provides a means for focusing and intensifying a certain aspect of our personal relationship with God, usually prayer. Abstinence sets aside even normal things that could distract us from a needed intensive seeking after God. And Jesus clearly expected that his followers would fast. However, it is once again possible to fast for the wrong reasons. Hypocritical fasting, or fasting in order to be seen as pious, was once again condemned. "Whenever you fast, **do not look** somber as the hypocrites do." While fasting may be an expression of repentance, or even of sorrow, drawing attention to our need for a more focused response on God eliminates the desired effect. Once again, Jesus emphasized his point with a bit of Rabbinic hyperbole. "...for they disfigure their faces to show others they are fasting." It's true that repenting "in sackcloth and ashes" was an ancient expression, but Jesus painted a picture of religious hypocrites so disfiguring their faces that they were unrecognizable. It is a picture of people putting on a show of fasting in order to receive recognition from others. "Truly I tell you, they have received their reward in full." Jesus stressed this conclusion by saying, "Amen, I say to you." In other words, this is very important, so listen closely. Those who express their relationship to God as hypocrites in order to be seen by others as pious will have received the only benefit they will gain as a result.

"But when you fast, **put oil** on your head and **wash** your face" (6:17). Here Jesus provided authoritative instructions, commands, about the right way to come to God with fasting. When you go out in public, take all the needed steps to look like you would any other day. Be sure to have a normal public appearance, "so that your fasting will not be noticed by men." In this way, "your Father who sees what is done in secret will reward you" (6:18). The Father is described as one who is "in secret." The Father sees everything, including the motivation of our hearts. A sincere heart-relationship with the Father will take into account the need to approach God in secret, in a way that cannot be seen by others. Only then will the desired benefit from God be experienced by the one sincerely seeking him.

These descriptions of a deeper relationship with the Father are very different from "normal" religious practices, either by the Pharisees of Jesus' day or by externally religious followers of Jesus in our day.

A Deeper Trust in the Father

Consistent communication is certainly the heart of any personal relationship. No relationship can be expected to flourish without a pattern of heart-to-heart communication. The glue that holds a relationship together is trust. And trust is a very fragile thing.

Trust must be earned, and trust can be broken. Yet, trust is so vitally important to any potentially intimate relationship it must be pursued at all costs. And that includes a deep, personal trust in the Lord. In fact, in many ways "faith" is really about trust. It is about our ability to trust God in any situation, no matter what.

For that reason, it is essential that we be able to examine our own trust or lack of trust in God. How do we know whether or not we really trust God? What are signs that our trust in God may not be as strong as we would like it to be? And how we can strengthen that trust? The rest of the Sermon in chapter six addresses those questions.

Jesus began by providing commands about the things we treasure. "**Do not store up** for yourselves treasures on earth, where moths and vermin destroy, and where thieves break in and steal. But **store up** treasures in heaven, where moths and vermin do not destroy, and where thieves do not break in and steal" (6:19-20). In those days, banks as we know them did not exist. The common folks tended to store up valuables by hiding them somewhere "safe," like a storage closet or even a hole in the ground. Obviously, none of these places where really safe, and were always subject to deterioration or theft. Yet, the fact that they were valued enough to be stored in that kind of way indicated the priorities of the person treasuring them.

Many of our trust issues with God are really about our values. We would like to think that God values the same things we do, and that God will provide them and protect them for us. Unfortunately, that is very far from the truth. In fact, in another place Jesus said, "What people value highly is detestable in God's sight" (Luke 16:15).

For that reason, "Where your treasure is, there your heart will be also" (6:21). It's hard to develop a heart relationship of trust in God when the things we value and treasure in our hearts are very different from the things God values. The things we seek after determines the course and direction of our lives. The things we value define our personal priorities. The more our heart matches the heart of God, the more we will share God's values and priorities, and the easier it will be to walk in a relationship of intimate trust in God.

Jesus used a common symbol for the human heart as the "eye." Our eyes are the means by which we focus on the things we value, and the same is ultimately true of the heart. Using the symbol of the eye, Jesus taught that if your eyes are "healthy," your whole body, your whole concrete self, "will be full of light" (6:22). This word for "healthy" means single or sincere. It can also mean generous. If your eye, if your heart has a single, healthy focus, it will result in your whole life being filled with light. However, if your eyes are "unhealthy," or evil, then you will walk in darkness. An "evil eye" was an eye that did not respond to the needs of others with mercy, compassion, and generosity. A wholehearted focus on relationship with the Lord will be seen in how others are treated. The primary focus of your life will reflect your values and priorities, and it will determine your commitments. It will not only provide a light for the course of your life, it will also be a source of light and blessing for others.

In the end, it's all about who you are committed to serving. Everybody is serving somebody. Most people are serving themselves, pursuing the things they value. For those who have a sincere desire to serve God, it is important to remember that you can't serve two masters; you can't have two Lords. You can only be truly devoted to one Lord. In a word, "You cannot serve both God and money" (6:24). Some translations use the literal Aramaic word "Mammon," a word that generally refers to possessions, the material objects we value and the means we use to obtain them. It's not so much that God values the absence of Mammon as it is a matter of the extent to which we serve it. Do we have possessions or do possessions have us? Do we treasure those material objects and the means of obtaining them so highly that we spend too much time and energy on them? Do we worry about them?

Which brings up the next authoritative word of Jesus in this teaching. "Therefore I tell you, **do not worry**" (6:25). Jesus used the word for "worry" six times in these sayings. Six times he stressed the need to not worry, to not be unduly concerned, to not be anxious or to have undue care about something. Being anxious and fearful is a natural response to situations that are dangerous or even stressful.

In fact, some people seem to have a short "anxiety fuse" in their brains. However, a pattern of anxiety is a problem that can be overcome. Fear tends to offset faith. Worry is often a sign of a lack of trust. Do we really believe that our lives are in God's hands? Do we trust God to, in the end, do what is best for our lives?

"**Do not worry** about your life." The word Jesus used for "life" (Greek *psuche*) describes the essence of our lives, even our souls. However, we tend to worry about the external, temporary aspect of our lives and not the eternal things. Jesus specified that we are not to worry about what we will eat or drink or about what we will wear. He instructed us to examine nature to see God's faithful care of birds and flowers. "**Look at** the birds...**See** how the flowers" (6:26, 28). It's obvious that God has provided sufficiently for his creation, that God cares for birds and flowers. "Are you not much more valuable than they?" (6:26). God created human beings in his own image, with divine purpose and eternal significance. Human beings are not here today and gone tomorrow. If God is committed to the faithful care of his birds and flowers, how much more is God committed to the care of people?

In the end, worry is an exercise in futility. "Can any one of you by worrying add a single hour to your life?" (6:27). "A single hour to your life" can also be translated, "a single cubit to your height." In other words, worry accomplishes nothing. It just keeps you from a faith response to God. It blocks the gratitude that provides a positive, thoughtful response to the normal challenges that come along the way.

Jesus also pointed out that worry reflects a way of thinking and living that falls short of a real, personal relationship with God. "For the pagans run after all these things" (6:32). Those who are not in a covenant relationship with the Lord live their lives in the pursuit of food and drink and clothing, of the symbols of success and significance. Those who know the Lord have a different perspective, a different set of values, for "your heavenly Father knows you need them." Those who pursue God are well aware that God understands all about the natural needs of his people, and he will provide for them appropriately.

So, what is the bottom line? "But **seek** first his kingdom and his righteousness, and all these things will be given to you as well" (6:33). Here is the challenge to consider what we really value, what our lives are committed to. It is the challenge to examine our priorities and who and what we are really serving. For the followers of Jesus, there are really two priorities, two things to pursue: God's rule and God's righteousness, the themes of the Sermon on the Mount. Those who do can then simply rest in their trust and confidence of God. They are liberated to be content and not anxious about the external, temporary elements of their lives. In fact, they won't even worry about tomorrow, "for tomorrow will worry about itself. Each day has enough trouble of its own" (6:34). After all, much of our anxiety is about what might be and not about the present moment. Just as with the request to "Give us today our daily bread," the committed follower of Jesus understands that life is to be lived one day at a time, that every day is a unique and special gift from the Father. Worrying about tomorrow is not only pointless, it shows we really don't understand the nature of life in God's Kingdom.

A Greater Righteousness Summarized

Jesus then provided beautiful and important summary teachings that touched on both the relationship with God and with others that characterize a follower of Jesus.

"**Do not judge**, or you too will be judged" (7:1). This is not a reference to being discerning or to making right judgments. Rather, it's all about having a critical, judgmental attitude toward others. Religious hypocrites can be very quick to make disparaging remarks about others they consider less pious, even communicating condemnation, leading to rejection and broken relationships. The hypocrisy of such an attitude should be obvious. It's also true that having that kind of attitude only invites others to return the favor.

This kind of hypocrite can actually offer to be of assistance to the one they are condemning as a cover for the reality of their self-righteousness. Jesus' view of that ploy was clear. "You hypocrite, first **take** the plank out of your own eye, and then you will see clearly to remove the speck from your brother's eye" (7:5). It's amazing how minor some of the criticisms can be, forgetting that an attitude of condemnation, expressions of rejection, and self-righteousness, are much bigger planks than any speck someone might have. Relationships in God's Kingdom are noted for humility and gentleness.

So, you might think that Jesus is simply very easy on everybody, until he says, "Do not give dogs what is sacred; do not throw your pearls to pigs" (7:6). When Jesus mentioned "dogs" don't think of cute, domesticated dogs. These were wild dogs who attacked, scavenged and ruined for a living. And we all know about pigs, that will eat anything and trample them into the mud in the process. In this case, these two animals were used to describe some people who are so committed to opposing the rule of God, the righteousness of God, and the Good News about the Kingdom, that attempting to reason with them would not only eventually result in a lack of response but even a mocking contempt for the Gospel and an attempt to destroy the influence of the Kingdom. "If you do, they may trample them under their feet, and turn and tear you to pieces." The first saying advocates an open, loving heart toward all. However, the second saying shows that the time may come when continuing to offer the "pearl" of the Kingdom will be fruitless and an unnecessary source of opposition and persecution.

Jesus then returned to the subject of prayer. A citizen of God's Kingdom can pray confidently, expecting that God always hears and is at work on the behalf of the one praying. That confidence is expressed by three commands. "**Ask** and it will be given you; **seek** and you will find; **knock** and the door will be opened to you" (7:7). These three imperatives paint a picture of increasing levels of intensity, if not desperation. "Asking" is a fairly calm request. "Seeking" is more determined. "Knocking" is willing to interrupt in order to be heard. You may have heard that these commands also use the present continuous tense, describing a lifestyle of prayer. "Keep on asking...keep on seeking...keep on knocking." It's similar to how Luke recorded the teachings of Jesus on prayer, providing a model prayer followed by a parable about a persistent widow who refused to be ignored (11:1-8).

A lifestyle of prayer is based on a clear understanding of the nature and character of God. Our God is not playing games with us, teasing us, disappointing us. A good and thoughtful human father would not do that to his kids, so why would anyone think God would treat his children that way? "If you, then, though you are evil, know how to give good gifts to those who ask him" (7:11). Our Father always has our best interests at heart, will always give us the things that are good for us. In fact, the account in Luke put it this way: "How much more will your Father in heaven give the Holy Spirit to those who ask him" (11:13).

Finally, Jesus summarized the greater righteousness of the Kingdom in profoundly important terms. In fact, some call this principle "the Golden Rule." "So in everything, **do** to others what you would have them do to you" (7:12). While this principle is common to many religions, Jesus stated it in a unique way. The famous first century Rabbi Hillel taught, "What is hateful to you, do not do to anyone else," In the East, Confucius taught, "Do not to others what you would not wish done to yourself." Hypocrates wrote, "First, do no harm." These ancient traditions stated the principle negatively. Don't treat others in a way that will harm them. Instead, Jesus stated the principle positively. Treat others in the way you would want them to treat you! Serve others in the way that will be helpful, not just in a way that avoids causing harm. This is the Law of Love, the way of the Kingdom of heaven.

This final principle summarizes everything Jesus had previously taught in the Sermon, and it concludes that teaching. The use of "therefore" at the beginning implies that this statement is the conclusion of the matter. And it's not just the conclusion of the principles of greater righteousness under God's rule, "this sums up the Law and the Prophets." Everything revealed in the Old Testament, when seen through the lens of the Kingdom righteousness Jesus came to establish, is summarized in this statement. How we treat others is the true test of our submission to the rule of God in our lives.

The Way of Obedience

Jesus had been teaching as a Rabbi, but so much more than a Rabbi. Jesus taught with authority, giving specific and concrete commands. He didn't want his audience to just hear and appreciate his words. He wanted them to be obeyed. In fact, a lack of obedience, not a lack of understanding, would result in something less than Kingdom participation. Jesus emphasized the need to put his words into action by describing four scenarios.

Narrow and Wide Gates. Jesus commanded his followers, "**Enter** through the narrow gates" (7:13). Contrasting the "two ways" was a common theme in Old Testament wisdom literature and also seen in some of the prophets. Jesus was contrasting two ways, one narrow and one wide. The wide gate and broad road were easy to find and walk on. In fact, it was the way most people chose, the path of least resistance. Unfortunately, that way "leads to destruction." On the other hand, the small gate and the narrow road, the one being provided by Jesus, "leads to life." Everyone is responsible to decide which road they want to walk on and which gate to use to gain entrance to that road. In another place, Jesus defined himself as "the gate" (John 10:7). He also said, "I am the way," and "no one comes to the Father except through me" (John 14:6). Jesus is the narrow gate and the narrow road that leads to life. Every other gate and every other road only ends in destruction.

True and False Prophets. Some go to great lengths to disguise themselves as true followers of Jesus, but they are not just hypocrites, they are actually wolves seeking to bring destruction into the flock. "**Watch out** for false prophets" (7:15). They may look like sheep, but they have a wolf's heart. A similar thing is true about trees. It doesn't matter how attractive they may look on the outside, there is a clear difference between a thorn bush and a fig tree. It's important to discern the kind and quality of fruit being borne by a person's life. What are the long-term results of their life and influence? Just looking good is not enough. Just having charisma is insufficient. It's important to test their character. "Thus, by their fruit you will recognize them" (7:20).

True and False Disciples. Just saying and doing things that seem to mark a genuine Jesus follower can be deceiving. It's possible to even outwardly confess Jesus as "Lord," and even to prophesy, drive out demons, and perform many miracles, all in the name of Jesus, and not be a true disciple. "Then I will tell them plainly, 'I never knew you. **Away** from me, you evildoers" (7:23). There are two problems with these so-called disciples. They practice lawlessness. Their lives do not match with their words. And Jesus does not "know" them, he does not have a real, personal, heart-to-heart relationship with them. And that means they don't really know him as well. In fact, if they did know Jesus, they would not be doers and workers of lawlessness.

Wise and Foolish Builders. A wise builder is someone who not only hears the words of Jesus but puts them into practice. He is a doer of the word and not just a hearer. On the other hand, a foolish builder actually hears the words of Jesus but does not put them into practice. He is not a doer of the word. He does not realize that Jesus is not just providing interesting and helpful ideas. Jesus is defining and prescribing a new Kingdom reality, a greater righteousness. As a result, the life of a wise builder will stand the test of time, will stand in the midst of the storms of life, while the life of a foolish builder, when faced with the storms of life, will fall "with a great crash." It is the total life-experience of someone building a life that will demonstrate whether or not obedience to the commands of Christ was the foundation of that building.

These four scenarios clearly communicated the authority of Jesus and the need to live out the meaning of his teachings. That element was unique to Jesus as a first century Jewish Rabbi. And the audience understood it. "The crowds were amazed at his teaching, because he taught as one who had authority, and not as their teachers of the law" (7:28-29). Jesus could not have taught with that authority if he had not been who he claimed to be, the Messiah, the King, the Son of the Living God. Jesus had and still has that authority. The test of our obedience can still be seen over the course of our lives. That is our challenge and our opportunity.

4 THE COMMAND TO TRUST

I'm drawn to the abstract, the theoretical. I have a love for the logical and the symmetrical. Unfortunately, that personality tendency could result in a purely theoretical approach to faith, to theology, to Jesus. It could even result in an abstract understanding and application of the commands of Jesus. But that would be a giant step in the wrong direction.

Jesus was all about relationship. He called certain men and women to follow him, to be his disciples, his apprentices, not just so they could memorize pithy sayings or start a new school of philosophy. I love how the gospel of Mark put it: "He appointed twelve that they might be with him" (3:14). He was looking for followers who would want to be with him, who would look forward to learning from him and sharing in his mission. "...and that he might send them out to preach."

On many occasions Jesus had opportunity to comment on the faith of his followers and of those receiving his ministry. He often commanded them to "believe" and drew attention to their "little faith." But for Jesus, the command to believe was not a command to accept certain propositional truths about him. Jesus wanted them to learn how to put their trust in him, to really believe that he was who he said he was, that he clearly understood the Father's will, and that he always had their best interests in mind. In the end, "faith" is a personal, relational response of trust in the Lord. It is also a response of loving obedience.

Loving Obedience

Jesus was the supreme example of loving obedience to the Father. For Jesus, love for the Father was not a feeling but rather a decision to serve and obey. To love someone in authority implies obedience. It's not possible to say we love God but refuse to obey him. Jesus modeled loving obedience, finally by going to the cross.

He began his mission by submitting himself to the public ministry of his cousin John. It must have been a shock when Jesus showed up to be baptized by John. The preaching of John had been very clear: his mission was to prepare the way for someone more powerful who would be able to "baptize with the Holy Spirit and fire." So, when Jesus came to be baptized by John, it is no wonder John objected. But Jesus responded in an authoritative way, in essence saying, "Just do it!" Do it now!

Why? Jesus' relationship of loving obedience with the Father gave him a clear understanding of the need "to fulfill all righteousness." Jesus was on a mission from the Father, committed to fulfilling that mission. The Father had sent John to prepare the way by preaching a repentance needed to prepare for an invasion of God's Kingdom, and while Jesus was the King, the public launching of his mission needed to conform to the purpose of the Father. It needed to be done right! Jesus needed to begin by acknowledging the importance of John's mission and using that mission as the launching pad for his own. It's no wonder that John simply consented to the command of Jesus.

The initial message of Jesus was then identical to John's: "Repent, for the kingdom of heaven has come near" (Matthew 3:2; 4:17). The command to repent was a central theme of the preaching of both John and Jesus. "**Repent**" (Greek *metanoeo*) was a word rich in meaning. For those of us who were raised in church, "repent" can simply mean "be sorry," and especially, "be sorry I got caught." But in the New Testament, "repent" literally means to have another mind, another perspective, another mindset. It refers to a radical change of mind that results in a change of conduct. Jesus is commanding his listeners to learn an entirely new way of thinking.

And specifically, a new way of thinking about "the kingdom of heaven." The rule of God, the domain of the King, simply describes everything that is under the control of God, everything that conforms to the character of God. To be under the rule of God means we have clearly identified ourselves with God, adopted God's values as our own, and committed ourselves to the will and purpose of God. The goal of the Kingdom citizen is to see the glory of God revealed in every situation.

Jesus was not just coming as the Messiah, he was coming as the King of God's Kingdom. And the coming of the Kingdom of heaven would ultimately change everything. Everything would be made new. Identifying as a citizen of God's Kingdom would mean more than "going to heaven when I die." It would mean completely new loyalties and priorities. It would call for a whole-hearted repentance.

Obedience to the commands of Jesus has to start with repentance. But then we will see the need to obey any and all of his commands, from the "big" ones to the "little" ones. I love how Matthew's Gospel shows specific examples of loving obedience being required of the disciples, even in mundane situations.

There was only one miracle of Jesus recorded in all four Gospels: the feeding of the five thousand. You remember the story. When a crowd gathered to hear Jesus teach, he spent the entire time teaching and healing their sick. When the disciples noticed that the folks had gotten hungry, and that they were not any restaurants nearby, they made a recommendation. "Send the crowds away, so they can go to the villages and buy themselves some food" (Matthew 14:15). Nice guys! Five thousand men, not counting women and children, starting to walk toward some village, any village, hoping to find something to eat?! Not a good plan!

Instead, Jesus had a different idea. And it didn't involve a suggestion, a committee meeting, or a vote. Jesus gave his followers two simple commands: "**You give** them something to eat" (verse 16). Don't just send them away; you serve them. You find them something to eat.

Of course, the disciples were quick to analyze the situation and determine that five loaves of flat bread and two sardines would barely feed a little boy let alone that crowd. Resulting in a second command: "**Bring** them here to me" (verse 18). They didn't need to understand what Jesus was thinking or what he was going to do. They just needed to obey. A simple act of loving obedience would put the situation in the hands of Jesus. They just needed to trust that Jesus knew what he was doing and would do the right thing.

Isn't that always the case with us in every situation?

Courageous Faith

Because faith is a response of relational trust in someone else, loving obedience can often be seen as a response to the command to believe. Out of context, "faith" can be theoretical and very difficult. In a relationship of trust and obedience, it is not so much a kind of "leap" as it is a response of love.

Many times, in the ministry of Jesus, a miraculous work was preceded by a command to believe, a call for courageous faith amid contradictions and obstacles. A willingness to simply trust despite appearances, invited the supernatural intervention of Jesus into a variety of situations. When the disciples observed how Jesus served in miraculous ways, they would learn how to do the same.

For instance, there was the case of the Roman Centurion who asked Jesus to heal his servant. This soldier had a great respect for authority and recognized the authority of Jesus. He apparently had a simple willingness to trust Jesus fully and to accept the word of Jesus at face value. When Jesus saw these things in the Centurion, he commented on his faith. "Truly I tell you, I have not found anyone in Israel with such great faith" (Matthew 8:10). I wonder if religious people have trouble finding religious reasons to not believe.

Jesus responded to the request with two simple commands: "**Go**" and "**Let it be**." His authoritative word, when responded to with unquestioning trust, would release God's healing power to the servant. "And his servant was healed at that moment" (8:13).

And then there was the story of "a woman who had been subject to bleeding for twelve years." I love the picture of this woman's faith. Her sickness had resulted in her being perpetually "unclean" in Jewish society. She was forbidden to make physical contact with anyone, including Jesus. And yet, her desperate, courageous faith moved her to press through the crowd in order to reach Jesus. She didn't care what it looked like or what it might cost her personally. She had such trust in Jesus she had concluded, "If I only touch his cloak, I will be healed" (Matthew 9:21).

Can you picture her pressing through the crowd and finally, getting down on her knees so she could touch the hem of Jesus' robe? It was not only loving trust, it was humility and persistence. When her touch got Jesus' attention, he gave her a very personal if not emotional command: "**Take heart**, daughter." "**Be of good courage**! Be of good cheer!" Be encouraged and rejoice!

Mark's account of this story pointed out that "Jesus realized that power had gone out from him" (5:30). Jesus had a personal sense that someone's touch had resulted in a release of healing virtue. It must have caused his own heart to rejoice. Then Jesus made an amazing statement. "Your faith has healed you" (Matthew 9:22). The intensity of her faith, her desperate and courageous faith, had touched Jesus in such a way as to result in her healing. "And the woman was healed at that moment."

What about the amazing story of Jesus walking on the water? There are several versions of this story in the Gospels. Matthew records the account of Jesus sending his followers out to cross the lake ahead of him. After most of the night was gone, these experienced sailors hadn't made much progress, "because the wind was against" them (Matthew 14:24). So, just before dawn Jesus decided to help them out and came walking to them on the water.

Matthew recorded that "they were terrified." While I'm not particularly superstitious, seeing a figure in the dim dawn light walking toward me on the water would have certainly given me pause. I would tend to think I was just seeing things. In either case, fear would have been the natural response.

The big problem with fear is this. While it may be only natural in certain circumstances, it has the tendency to offset faith. A response of loving trust is hindered by a response of fear. In order for Jesus to show his followers his authority in this situation, he had to deal with their fear first. He had to give them a command to believe. "**Take courage**. It is I. **Don't be afraid**" (14:27). The command to "take courage" was the same word Jesus spoke to the woman who had touched the hem of his garment. In this case, Jesus had to add a second command to stop being afraid. They had to get control of their fear in order to see Jesus in the midst of this situation.

The only way for them to deal with their fear was to focus on the one addressing them. "It is I." It's interesting that this statement in the text is (Greek) *ego eimi*, or literally, "I am." Jesus was revealing himself as the one who has all authority. If they could fix their eyes on him, the fear would fade and the ability to trust would replace it. And not just a general faith, but a faith that saw Jesus for who he really is. "Truly you are the Son of God" (14:33).

ᗢ

Matthew seemed to like stories that show the ability of non-Jews to have a real, personal faith in Jesus. After all, the universal Kingdom mission of Jesus is one of Matthew's main themes. So, in addition to the Roman Centurion he also recorded the story of the Canaanite woman. When Jesus decided to take a break, he traveled with his disciples to the area of Tyre and Sidon in modern Lebanon. He may have thought he would get some rest away from the crowds in Galilee. While enjoying a pleasant meal with the boys, a local girl noticed him and decided to plead her case with him.

She knew she had no basis for asking anything of a Jewish Rabbi. However, her heart was hurting for her beloved daughter. As she put it, "My daughter is demon-possessed and suffering terribly" (Matthew 15:22). She wasn't just making a calm case for her daughter, she was "crying out." Her deep love for her daughter gave her the courage to approach this Jewish miracle-working prophet. She didn't ask Jesus to heal her daughter. She just said, "Have mercy on me." Somehow, she had confidence in the mercy and compassion of Jesus, leading her to believe that he would do the right thing by her daughter.

But how desperate was this mother? How persistent was her trust in the compassion of Jesus? How easily would she just give up and go her way?

Her first obstacle was the response of the disciples. After all, they were on vacation. There seemed to be no end to needy, clingy people. This Canaanite woman should just leave them alone. "Send her away." She's getting on our nerves. "She keeps crying out after us."

Her second obstacle was the apparent sense of Jewish entitlement coming from this Rabbi. "I was sent only to the lost sheep of Israel." You're not a part of my mission. I need to keep focused.

But rather than being discouraged, this mother became even more persistent. "Lord, help me!" How often have we prayed that prayer! We have no where else to turn.

To demonstrate the quality of her faith, Jesus restated the priority of his ministry to Israel, by saying, "It is not right to take the children's bread and toss it to the dogs." The ministry of Jesus, both the words and the works, belonged to Israel, the children of God. This Canaanite woman had not been invited to the Messianic banquet.

But rather than taking offense, this dear mother responded with a humble confidence in the Rabbi from Nazareth. "Even the dogs eat the crumbs that fall from the master's table." With this remarkable response, the Canaanite woman acknowledged that she was not an equal participant in the banquet. She also acknowledged that it wouldn't take more than a crumb to heal her daughter. And she acknowledged that the one serving the meal was the Master.

It's no wonder Jesus gave the command that resulted in a miracle. "Your request **is granted**" (15:28). In doing so, Jesus commented on the quality of her faith. "You have great faith." Her faith was humble and persistent. Her faith had been combined with her compassion for her daughter and her confidence in the compassion of Jesus. "And her daughter was healed at that moment."

Jesus Alone

The command to believe is very much dependent on a clear focus on the person of Jesus. It's not about religious conviction or mental assent to religious ideas. Seeing Jesus alone is the key to our ability to exercise effective faith.

No story illustrates that better than the account of Jesus and three of his disciples on the Mount of Transfiguration. After Jesus was acknowledged to be "the Christ, the Son of the Living God," and Jesus had predicted his death in chapter 16, chapter 17 opens on top of a high mountain. Jesus took Peter, James and John with him, and on the mountain, "he was transfigured before them." What a mind-blowing, life-changing experience that must have been. We really don't know all the details about what was happening and why it was happening. We are just told that "his face shone like the sun, and his clothes became white as the light." Surely the glory of God was being revealed in a unique way. The true nature of Jesus as the Son of God was shining through. While Jesus was fully human, a poor Rabbi from Nazareth, he was so much more than that. And now three of his followers were given a glimpse of his eternal glory and radiance.

Matthew also recorded that Moses and Elijah appeared and were talking with Jesus. Luke's Gospel recorded something about their conversation. "They spoke about his departure, which he was about to bring to fulfillment at Jerusalem" (9:31). They weren't discussing his glory but rather his upcoming death. They may have even discussed the significance of his death at Jerusalem. The word Luke used for "departure" means "exodus," and could have suggested the new exodus Jesus was going to accomplish for his people through his death.

What an amazing experience! So how did the disciples react? Leave it to Peter to speak out. "Lord, it is good for us to be here. If you wish, I will put up three shelters – one for you, one for Moses, and one for Elijah." Peter was having a religious experience, and he didn't want it to end. His declaration of "I will" showed that he was not so much contemplating the glory being revealed as he was wanting to take charge and find a way to preserve his experience. And his focus was not just on Jesus, but also on Moses and Elijah. He offered to build shelters for all three of them – and missed the point completely.

Fortunately, rather than the Father losing patience with these religious disciples, he spoke audibly out of the glory cloud. "This is my Son, whom I love; with him I am well pleased. **Listen** to him!" The Father was not interested in their religious experience or their religious need to honor the past by building shelters for Moses and Elijah. The Father wanted them to see Jesus! The Father wanted them to listen to Jesus! Everything else depended on that.

Hearing God's voice was a powerful corrective for these three men. "When the disciples heard this, they fell face down to the ground, terrified." Their reaction was worship, but it was also raw fear. They must have known that the Father was correcting them while making it very clear that their focus was to be on Jesus. Lying on the ground they were not aware that Moses and Elijah had returned to heaven and that the cloud of glory was gone. They must have just been shaking there on the ground, wondering how far God was going to go in correcting them. That's when Jesus came to them with two commands. "**Get up**" and "**Don't be afraid**" (17:7). The need to listen to Jesus had just been confirmed in a powerful, supernatural way. Jesus could have said anything to them and I have a feeling they would have quickly obeyed. Instead, the authoritative word of Jesus was intended to strengthen them.

An action was needed. "Get up." And an adjustment to their reaction was called for. "Stop being afraid." Their reaction had swung from one extreme to the other – from an offer to do what it took to maintain the glory of their religious experience to a fear that it was all over for them. While "the fear of the Lord" is always the beginning of wisdom, these men were afraid for their lives, and a self-centered, self-preserving fear always works against faith. Now they needed to refocus and get back to the mission.

Coming down from the mountain they encountered the other disciples trying (unsuccessfully) to cast a demon out of a boy. When Jesus saw their attempts to exorcise this demon, his response was rather harsh. "You unbelieving and perverse generation" (17:17). Jewish exorcists were not uncommon in that day. I can imagine that these disciples had been attempting to use the methods prescribed by those exorcists. I'm sure there may have been all kinds of mumbo jumbo and dancing around involved. All ineffective. One thing was lacking – real faith.

When Jesus rebuked the demon resulting in its hasty exit, the disciples asked why their efforts had been so unsuccessful. "Because you have so little faith." They didn't need more faith in their religious rituals and procedures. They needed to put all their confidence in the person and authority of Jesus. Deliverance procedures were just so much craziness without a clear focus on Jesus.

Real faith in Jesus, a genuine confidence in Jesus as God's authorized Son, would have sent the demon packing. With their eyes focused on Jesus, their faith would have been authoritative and powerful. In fact, Jesus put words of authority in the mouths of the believing. "If you have faith as small as a mustard seed, you can say to this mountain, '**Move** from here to there,' and it will move. Nothing will be impossible for you" (17:20). They didn't need more faith in their religious rituals. They didn't need more faith in their faith. They needed a simple faith in Jesus, with a focus on Jesus as the means and the end of every situation. With that clear focus, the supernatural would be available to them, working with them to confirm the truth about Jesus.

Matthew chapter 17 recorded another very interesting story about the authority of Jesus and the need for simple obedience to believe and act on his word. Jesus had an interesting conversation with Peter about the need to pay the temple tax. The tax collectors had specifically asked whether or not Jesus paid the tax, to which Peter replied, "Yes, he does." So, when Peter approached Jesus about the need to pay the tax, Jesus started the conversation with a question. "From whom do the kings of the earth collect duty and taxes – from their own children or from others?"

In this case, the tax in question was intended to support the expenses of temple worship. In essence, Jesus was asking whether or not, in theory, God was asking his Son to pay a tax to support the temple or was God asking it of others. Jesus really wanted to know if Peter was convinced that Jesus was God's Son. It didn't really matter whether or not Jesus thought the temple tax was legitimate, he just wanted to dialog with Peter on the subject.

Peter rightly responded, "From others." "Then the children are exempt," Jesus replied. So, if he was God's Son, he shouldn't be required to pay the tax. It wasn't that Jesus objected to paying taxes, he just wanted to explore Peter's thinking on how it might pertain to God's Son.

I can easily imagine it left Peter scratching his head. He had a simple question about paying the tax and Jesus wanted to engage him in an abstract conversation. And so, Jesus ended the discussion with a simple command. "**Take** the first fish you catch; open its mouth and you will find a four-drachma coin. Take it and give it to them for my tax and yours" (17:27). Jesus didn't want to create an unnecessary controversy, so he decided to confirm his status as God's Son by performing a miracle in the provision for the temple tax.

Although the story doesn't end with a conclusion, I'm assuming that Peter went fishing, opened the mouth of the first fish he caught, and found the exact change to pay the temple tax – not only for Jesus but for Peter as well. All that was required was obedience to the command of Jesus. Even more so, this encounter called for a deep faith and confidence that Jesus was who he claimed to be – the very Son of God.

Come!

I don't want to leave the subject of the command of Jesus to believe in him before revisiting the story in Matthew chapter 14. You'll remember that Jesus came to the disciples in the boat, walking on the water. Because they thought they were seeing a ghost, Jesus commanded them to be courageous and to stop being afraid. When the wind died down, the disciples concluded, "Truly you are the Son of God." Jesus wasn't showing off, he was revealing himself to his friends in a way that would strengthen and deepen their faith in him.

In the middle of this story is a strange event. Peter decided to design his own unique test to see whether or not this apparition was Jesus. "If it's you...tell me to come to you on the water." What was Peter thinking! What kind of a test was that? Did Peter think that if it turned out to be Jesus, he wouldn't ask for such a ridiculous demonstration? Was Peter hoping for an exceptionally interesting spiritual experience if it was Jesus and he decided to take him up on this crazy suggestion?

Who knows? All we know is that Jesus issued a one-word command: **"Come!"** (14:29). That one authoritative word of command from Jesus had the power to enable Peter to walk on that water, if he really was ready to give it a try.

And sure enough, "Peter got down out of the boat, walked on the water and came toward Jesus." Case closed. Jesus was who he claimed to be. Peter didn't need a sophisticated theological explanation. He just needed to hear and obey the simple command of Jesus.

Oh, if it were only that simple! "When he saw the wind, he was afraid, and beginning to sink, [he] cried out." An initial decision to believe in Jesus and obey his word was enough to get Peter out of the comfort of his boat and to start walking supernaturally on the water. But it would take something more to sustain his watery walk-about. Now he would need to learn the all-important need to keep his eyes on Jesus, no matter the storm or the obstacles. That kind of faith is a daily growing and strengthening progress, with good days and bad.

At least Peter knew the right prayer. "Lord, save me." I don't know about you, but even though I have loved and trusted the Lord from an early age, there are still days and circumstances when I need to pray, "Lord, save me." I never seem to outgrow my need for the Lord's saving mercy.

A less merciful Lord would have let Peter thrash about in the water for a while, maybe "to teach him a lesson." Instead, "Immediately Jesus reached out his hand and caught him." Although Jesus then spoke to Peter about the need for his faith to grow, he didn't let him flounder. He didn't let him drown.

I can see Jesus reaching out his hand, pulling Peter out of the water, and holding him close while they returned to the boat. I know I can count on Jesus to do that for me during the many times when I need him.

Disciples of Jesus, those who have adopted the yoked life, are learning to hear and obey his command to believe. It calls for an attitude of loving obedience as well as courageous faith. It requires us to see Jesus alone and to keep our eyes on him, no matter how strong the wind blows against us. Learning to obey this one command will be an important key to our apprenticeship in God's Kingdom.

5 SERMON ON THE MISSION

Followers of Jesus are very aware of the fact that they have signed up to be on mission with Jesus. They have signed up to be committed, lifelong apprentices to Jesus, and that means being with him where he is and sharing in whatever he is doing.

Jesus came on a mission from the Father. In fact, that mission is still very much in effect. As the King of the Kingdom of heaven, Jesus launched the mission of God and established a Kingdom embassy to carry on that mission throughout the earth, to faithfully engage in the mission until "the full harvest" has been brought in.

After his resurrection, Jesus made the assignment to his followers clear. "As the Father has sent me, I am sending you" (John 20:21). Not only were they to carry on the mission and to extend it throughout the earth, they were also commissioned to recruit and train other apprentices, by baptizing and teaching them. Apprentices raising up apprentices to advance God's Kingdom in every generation.

The disciples were to be disciple-makers, and it was assumed that they would be living the "yoked life" while calling others to come under the yoke of their Master Jesus.

At the end of Matthew's ninth chapter, we hear Jesus giving missional instructions in another way. He modeled the mission in 9:35-36, teaching, preaching and healing. His heart response to the crowds was one of compassion, "because they were harassed and helpless, like sheep without a shepherd." They needed what Jesus came to bring.

He then turned to his disciples and said, "The harvest is plentiful but the workers are few. **Ask** the Lord of the harvest, therefore, to send out workers into the harvest field" (9:37-38). What the disciples didn't realize was that the prayer for workers was to be first answered by them. They were the workers who needed to extend the mission of God into the harvest field being presented to them.

That sets the stage for the great Sermon on the Mission in Matthew chapter 10. Jesus began by appointing 12 of his disciples to be "apostles" (the only time in Matthew where this word is found). There were many more disciples of Jesus than these 12, but they were appointed to be authoritative agents of the King and his Kingdom. In ancient Greek and Roman cultures, an "apostle" was sent by a government to be the ambassador to a certain area, authorized to establish an official embassy and represent the government in the new area. Ultimately, these official embassies were to spread the influence of their culture and language to the surrounding people and cities.

So, Jesus authorized 12 of his disciples to be his "apostles." They did not represent themselves but the King and his government who authorized who was authorizing their mission. They were not to function with their own authority but with the authority Jesus was giving them.

And notice the authority Jesus gave his apostles. "Jesus…gave them authority to drive out impure spirits and to heal every disease and sickness" (10:1). Jesus had just modeled his mission to them. Motivated by "compassion" as "shepherds," the apostles were to begin sharing in the mission of Jesus. But not without more specific instructions.

Commentators have noted that the Sermon on the Mission has three distinct sections, each concluding with an "amen saying," 10:5-15, 16-23, and 24-42. They have also noticed that the first instructions were clearly aimed at the immediate mission of these apostles, while the later instructions seemed to have broader, more universal relevance to the ongoing mission of God.

The Command to Go

Jesus started by giving the apostles seven commands in rapid order (verses 6-8). Jesus was obviously serious about the mission, not just providing advice and wise instructions but giving authoritative orders to those going out.

"**Go** to the lost sheep of Israel." The mission was to begin "with the Jew first," God's covenant people. It would ultimately extend to everyone, everywhere, but needed to start at home. "**Proclaim** the message, 'The kingdom of heaven is near.'" These were the first words of the Gospel from both John and Jesus. The King had arrived, and along with him, the domain of the King, the authority of heaven breaking in and being established on the earth. "**Heal** the sick," the weak and suffering needing care and a cure. "**Raise** the dead," demonstrating the eternal life that had come with the Kingdom. "**Cleanse** those who have leprosy," bringing good news and health to those considered "unclean" in society. "**Drive out** demons," demonstrating the authority of the Kingdom of heaven over every element of the kingdom of darkness. "**Freely give**," recognizing that every good and perfect gift comes from the rule of God and is to be freely shared with others.

These mission commands summarize the essence of the mission of God being launched by Jesus. In point of fact, I have taught in Bible College and Seminary for many years, and I have rarely attempted to teach students how to obey these commands. We teach church government and church administration. We teach hermeneutics and homiletics. But, if we are to faithfully carry on the mission of God in our time and place, we need the authority of Jesus along with clear instructions on what establishing a Kingdom embassy might look like. "For the kingdom of God is not a matter of talk but of power" (1 Corinthians 4:20).

After giving the apostles the core Kingdom assignment, Jesus added six specific commands relevant to their immediate mission. "**Search** for some worthy person in whatever town or village you enter" (10:11). Discern who is ready to hear and respond to the Gospel of the Kingdom. "**Stay** at their house." Hospitality was (and is) a very important part of Eastern culture. The privilege of extending hospitality to an emissary of the King would result in a great blessing to that household. "**Give it your greeting**," "peace to this household, may the shalom of God rest on you." "Let your peace **rest** on it". However, if it turns out that the members of that household are not receptive to the message or the messenger, in fact, they may prove to be hostile to God and his Messiah, "let your peace **return** to you." That home and family just robbed themselves of a blessing. In fact, if no one in that home or even the entire town is willing to welcome the messengers and their message, "**shake** the dust off of your feet" (10:11-14) as a sign that you are leaving them behind. They have left you no choice but to commit them to the justice of God.

The immediate mission Jesus sent his apostles on was a local, short-term assignment. The instructions of Jesus communicated an almost emergency need to invite as many as possible and as quickly as possible to join them as apprentices of Jesus. I'm sure Jesus knew that by the end of that generation, the Roman army would invade the land and destroy Jerusalem and the temple. The time had come to offer salvation to their Jewish kinsmen.

At the same time, any apostolic mission requires a sense of urgency. The salvation of an entire people is at stake. In the end, the judgment of God is at stake. It is vital that all the people receive a good-faith opportunity to embrace the Gospel and to acknowledge the King. The mission of God is just as important today as it was to those first apostles.

The Command to Be On Guard

In verses 16-23, Jesus followed up with some instructions that anticipated the future mission of the apostles and of the early apostolic church. In these instructions, Jesus gave them warnings as well as predictions. The revolutionary nature of their Kingdom mission would result in opposition and persecution, so they needed to be on guard.

Jesus saw his disciples sharing his mission as sheep among wolves. As I'm sure you know, being compared to a sheep is not necessarily a compliment. Sheep are obedient but also vulnerable. They are easily exploited and scared away. On the other hand, the field of the world is full of unscrupulous, manipulative, even hostile wolves, looking for "easy-pickings" sheep. For that reason, Jesus gave the apostles (and us) an interesting word of advice.

Jesus commanded them to "**be** as shrewd as snakes and as innocent as doves" (10:16). Jesus wasn't so much calling his disciples "snakes" and "doves" as he was drawing attention to certain characteristics of those animals. He was commanding them to be "shrewd," to be sensible, thoughtful, to have a carefully calculated awareness of others, to have a practical wisdom, to be circumspect in their view of others. He also commanded them to be "innocent," pure, without guile or any attempt to deceive or misrepresent either themselves, the Gospel or the Kingdom of God.

These two character qualities almost seem contradictory. Most would consider shrewdness to require a certain amount of guile, of cleverness. On the other hand, it's not uncommon for people to view the "innocent" as naive, even a bit dull. But there is more to these two terms than the either/or of guile versus naivete. Jesus advised the need for both, and so it's possible for an apprentice of Jesus to be both. Jesus was discerning, wise, and astute in his shrewdness while remaining harmless, innocent, and transparent in his guilelessness.

Jesus followed this command with a command to "**be on your guard**" (10:17). If they were to be fulfilling an apostolic assignment in wolf country, they would need to be aware of the possibility of active persecution. They would need to give attention to that possibility, to be on guard for that possibility, without being fearful or timid. They would be wise to be realistic about the nature of their Kingdom mission.

We know that Jesus came as the King, establishing the authority of his Kingdom on the earth. And we know that at the end of the age, the Kingdom of God will be the only Kingdom left standing. In the meantime, there are two very different kingdoms co-existing on planet earth, in constant conflict over the fate of the human inhabitants. Two citizenships, two loyalties, two destinies offered to everyone who is born during this period of time. For that reason, there is continual warfare between the two kingdoms. However, the kingdoms wage war in very different ways. The two kingdoms define victory in very different ways. So, the apostles then and now are to anticipate encountering opposition, even severe opposition, as they carry on their mission.

Jesus told these men, and really the first generation of preachers, that they would end up being flogged in Jewish synagogues because of their message. They would be arrested and brought before authorities to answer for their "crimes." However, they wouldn't be alone. Their mission was not just a human mission but the mission of God. The Holy Spirit would be with them, sharing in every aspect of the mission. The Holy Spirit would actually give them the words to say when they found themselves on trial (10:20).

It's not that the Holy Spirit would show up as needed to bail them out. They had been following the lead of the Holy Spirit every step of the way, and for that reason, could rely on a very specific partnership with the Holy Spirit, even (if not especially) in the context of persecution.

The severity of the conflict between the two kingdoms would result in human division, even in families. Those who were hindered by a fear of rejection should deal with that first, because faithfulness to the mission would result in some people actually hating them, and ultimately putting them to death.

At least Jesus was honest and clear up front about the nature of the mission, of the cost of discipleship. It makes you wonder why anyone has actually accepted the assignment. It seems like a far cry from "just repeat this prayer after me and you're in."

The fact is, we simply believe that Jesus is who he claimed to be. We believe the message and are committed, loyal citizens of God's Kingdom! We have a life-or-death message, one with eternal consequences.

Spreading the Good News of the Kingdom, extending the influence of the

Kingdom to every corner of the earth in every generation, is always the dire need of the moment. That's why Jesus commanded his apostles that, when they found themselves in a place that was simply committed to persecuting them, they were to "**flee** to another" place. Don't take too much time to defend yourself or to wonder why people are rejecting the message. It's time to move on and give another place and another people an opportunity to hear the announcement of the Kingdom and decide whether or not they want to declare their loyalty to the King.

Jesus then provided some general instructions concerning the mission in 10:24-42. Any ambassador of King Jesus on mission for his King will be interested in these principles and promises.

Understand that when you are a personal representative of King Jesus, you should not expect to be treated any better than he had been. If they called him a devil, don't be surprised if they have less than flattering things to call you.

And refuse to be intimidated by those who oppose the Rule of God. In fact, be bold with your announcement of the Good News. Jesus had been personally teaching his disciples words of life and liberation, many of them in private. Now he commanded them to "**speak**" those things out in the open, in the daylight. They were even commanded to "**proclaim**" those things they had heard from Jesus publicly and boldly from the rooftops. They would have had a constant need for boldness and liberty of speech as they would carry out their assigned mission.

The presence of boldness acknowledged the ongoing challenge of fear. Three of the final commands given by Jesus in the Sermon on the Mission address this problem. Twice Jesus commanded his ambassadors, "**Do not be afraid**" (10:28, 31). I have heard it said (though I haven't counted them myself) that the command to "fear not" is found 365 times in the Bible, one for each day of the year. There is no question that fear is a common, instinctive response on the part of human beings. Stepping out in obedience to the instructions of Jesus can't wait for fear to disappear. It has to be faced, challenged, and defeated with the shield of faith. Boldness does not imply the absence of fear, but rather a willingness to face fear down and declare the word of the Lord by faith.

In general, there are two kinds of fear. Natural, human fear is a defensive reaction, a warning to pay attention and consider the need to fight or run away. This kind of fear is all about looking out for myself, protecting myself, defending myself.

A more unnatural fear is the "fear of the Lord." The fear of the Lord sees God at the center of every situation, factors God into every decision, always puts God and God's will first. It is a God-centered approach to life. It's no wonder that Jesus also commanded his followers, "Rather, **be afraid** of the One who can destroy both soul and body in hell" (10:28). Facing our natural self-preserving fear and focusing on God at the center of every situation will empower boldness and enable the accomplishment of the mission, no matter how dangerous the assignment.

This is particularly true in light of the predictions of Jesus in this sermon. Jesus emphasized the need to acknowledge and be personally loyal to him. He stated that the effect of his mission was to bring a sword rather than peace. Human beings would be divided between those loyal to Jesus and those who are not. In this context, true disciples will need to take up their own cross in the light of the cross of Christ and follow him, no matter what the cost. Gaining the kind of life Jesus is making available will necessitate giving up a normal self-centered life.

On the other hand, those who welcome the disciples and embrace their message will be rewarded. It's no wonder that "the fear of man" will tend to dilute and compromise the mission. The "fear of the Lord" will prove to be absolutely essential.

The Command to Follow

The Sermon on the Mission provides vitally important instructions for all apprentices of Jesus. Everyone living the yoked life is committed to the assignment of recruiting and training other apprentices while establishing powerful Kingdom embassies throughout the world in every generation. Believing in Jesus is not just about going to heaven when we die. At some point in time every faithful follower must settle the issue: God is my Father and heaven is my home – period! Now let's get on with the reason why we are still alive sucking air on planet earth. There is work to be done – an assignment to fulfill. The purpose of our lives after salvation is not to celebrate our new-found fire insurance while hoping not to make too many mistakes before we die. We have a purpose. We are on a mission.

This essential theme is not just confined to the tenth chapter of Matthew. Throughout Matthew's Gospel we see Jesus commanding various people to leave everything behind and follow him. Dietrich Bonhoeffer referred to this as "the cost of discipleship." Jesus simply commanded those contemplating becoming his apprentice to "count the cost."

At one time, a teacher of the Law approached Jesus with the offer to become one of his followers. Jesus tried to discourage him by being direct about the price he would have to pay. Their accommodations might be even poorer than those of foxes. They may have to leave normal social duties behind to follow him. The command of Jesus was very simple, clear and straightforward. "Follow me" (8:22).

The command to "follow" seemed almost harsh. It implied that Jesus would always be leading the way. Those following would be considered his personal attendants. They would have to be committed to taking his side on every issue, to do everything they could to stay close to him, to conform wholly to his example. Jesus was calling for a "following" lifestyle, a deep and determined commitment to being close by his side, no matter what the cost.

These words, this command, was the way Jesus recruited his disciples. When he encountered Matthew collecting taxes, his command, and his expectation was clear. "Follow me" (9:9).

In some cases, following Jesus meant leaving other things. When the disciples reported to Jesus that the Pharisees had been offended by his words, he commanded them to *leave* them (15:14). They couldn't have it both ways. To follow Jesus meant to follow him alone.

When teaching his disciples about the cost of following him, he had to actually rebuke them for objecting to his harsh demands. Peter objected to the statement of Jesus that his mission would ultimately lead to his death. Jesus responded with a command. "*Get* behind me, Satan" (16:23). It wasn't that Peter was demon possessed. His error, one reinforced by the self-centered perspective of the kingdom of darkness, was to focus on human concerns rather than the concerns of God. The mission of God was not about self-preservation but rather redemption.

To emphasize this point Jesus followed up with three commands. Those wanting to be disciples of Jesus, those truly committed to following him, would have to *deny* themselves, *take up* their cross and *follow* him. The word Jesus used for "self-denial" meant that the disciples would be expected to behave in a wholly selfless manner. They were to refuse recognition, to give up the limelight in order to follow Jesus. Taking up their cross could only be understood in the light of the cross of Christ. Following Jesus would be a life poured out, a life for others. Once again, Jesus concluded his call to discipleship with the words, "Follow me" (16:24). It's no wonder so few committed themselves to a lifestyle of discipleship!

On another occasion, a man – sometimes referred to as a "rich young ruler" – approached Jesus with a question. "Teacher, what good thing must I do to get eternal life?" (19:16). Looking back, it seems like an arrogant if not appalling question. What did he mean by "good thing"? Who did he propose "doing" such a good thing? How could he think it possible to "get" eternal life?

The first response of Jesus was to command to *keep* the commandments. If he truly embraced the commandments of God, he would come to know the heart and purpose of God, the spirit of the law. They would lead him to a knowledge of Christ and a commitment to the mission of Christ. However, this guy was just trying to justify himself. So, Jesus forced him to face his issue head on with four commands. If he were really committed to a mature, complete conformity to the spirit of the law, he would have to *go*, *sell* his possessions, *give* the proceeds to the poor, and yes, you guessed it, "**Follow** me" (19:21).

This young man had confessed that he had kept the commandments, "You shall not murder, you shall not commit adultery, you shall not steal, you shall not give false testimony, you shall honor your father and mother," and beside that he had kept the commandment to "love your neighbor as yourself." But the spirit of the law went beyond an external conformity to a moral code. In fact, the ten commandments included, "you shall not covet," don't desire what your neighbor has. Be content. Be a giver, not a taker. Somehow the moral character of God hadn't gone beyond a surface level in this man. There was a factor that had to be rooted out for him to be a sincere, devoted follower of Christ. He would not be able to serve God and Mammon. He would need to be radically liberated of his love of material things, his love of wealth and the status that came with it, if there was any chance of him taking up his cross and following Jesus.

I suspect there is a root hindrance in every one of us, something that has to die in order truly live with and for Christ.

The Command to Be Prepared

It is so important to see that God always has a plan. Our God is a God of purpose and of order. The mission of God to establish the influence of Kingdom embassies in the world is only possible when the apprentices of Jesus become aware, not only of God's mission but also of God's plan, of God's purpose.

I must confess that I am a compulsive planner. It's almost like being a compulsive chess player, seeing all possible moves in advance. I always have a Plan A and a Plan B, and just in case, a Plan C. Being a planner definitely has its advantages. But there's just one problem with that "gift": my Plan A is almost never God's Plan

A. And part of the curse of being a compulsive planner is the tendency to get irritated when a plan doesn't work out. "I love it when a plan comes together."

I believe the ability to plan is, in fact, a gift from God. But the Kingdom of God is not dependent on our giftedness. There must always be a determination to patiently wait and discern God's plan. There is too much at stake to just draw up some clever plan and then launch it, hoping God will bless our plans. But how often do we do that very thing?

So, I can plan, but I must always hold those plans loosely, waiting for God to confirm his specific plans, God's specific Kingdom assignment as I seek to participate in God's mission.

Our primary responsibility is not to make final plans but simply to be prepared. God calls us to be alert, to be watchful and attentive. God calls us to be ready to move and act when God gives the signal.

It reminds me of the story of Jesus instructing the disciples to prepare for his final entrance into Jerusalem. Jesus had all the details in mind beforehand. He began by commanding the disciples to "**go** into the village" to make preparations (21:2). Jesus knew that as soon as they entered the village, they would find a donkey with her colt tired up. He instructed them to untie the donkey and her colt, tricky business at best, and bring them to him. But what if the owner objected? They were simply to respond that "the Lord needs them," and the owner would command the donkey and her colt to go immediately.

I love how Jesus instructed the disciples to speak for "the Lord." This was a huge claim, one that went beyond a Messianic claim. Jesus was now clearly declaring himself to be "the Lord," and that he knew that the owner of the livestock also recognized his lordship.

In fact, there was no way Jesus could have known all of these details in advance without being the Lord.

Jesus had a plan, and the responsibility of the disciples was simply to obey the instructions given them and to make all preparations for the Lord to act.

It is a high honor to be able to participate on any level in God's Kingdom mission. To make any contribution, to provide any service, is a high privilege. Even the strongest, most assertive leader must understand the nature of the yoked life. There is only one King in God's Kingdom. There is only one Lord. All the rest of us are servants, seeking to be obedient and faithful. In fact, that is the only way we will bear the intended fruit as Kingdom ambassadors.

Being on mission with Jesus is our ultimate assignment as his apprentices. We are called to recruit and train new apprentices wherever we go, but our effectiveness will depend on the extent to which we ourselves are living the yoked life. We can't reproduce true disciples without being one, and that requires a lifestyle of preparedness and loving obedience, preparing the way for the King to come and act.

6 THE COMMAND TO RECEIVE SALVATION

Growing up in an evangelical church I often heard the question, "Are you saved?' and the statement, "Jesus saves." It seemed like salvation was primarily a matter of getting my fire insurance before I died. All I had to do was repeat "the prayer" and the threat of hell was no longer in my future.

But when we examine the immense subject of salvation in Scripture, we see that it means a whole lot more than that. When we consider Jesus as our Savior, we need to see all he came to save us from, and the price he had to pay to buy that for us.

It might help to take a moment to do a little word study. The (Greek) word in the New Testament for "salvation" is *sozo*. It is a beautiful, large word with a wide range of meaning. It means to preserve or be rescued. It means to bring out safely from a dangerous situation. *Sozo* means to free someone from disease or oppression. It means to keep or preserve something in good condition. It also means to thrive, prosper, and get on well. This wonderful word is translated in a variety of ways: save, heal, make whole, do well.

So, when we think of Jesus as our Savior and examine his work of salvation, we see examples of deliverance from unclean spirits and the healing of diseases. Ultimately, we see Jesus healing the destructive effects of sin, starting with the forgiveness of sins, his greatest act of salvation.

In every case, salvation was connected to an authoritative word. A word that needed to be received and acted on by faith.

Matthew's Gospel contains five sermons, five compilations of the sayings of Jesus, organized topically. In between these sermons are stories. These stories illustrate the meaning of Jesus's teachings and set the stage for the next sermon. The authoritative words of Jesus in chapters 5-7 are followed by stories about the authoritative works of Jesus in chapters 8-9. The stories then set the stage for the next sermon in chapter 10. So, it's no wonder we find many of the stories about the work of Jesus to save in chapters 8-9. Although these chapters do not contain authoritative instructions to the disciples, they illustrate the authoritative word and work Jesus was entrusting to them.

The Command of Deliverance

We American Christians don't think a lot about demons, unless it's in the context of the occult or a scary movie. Fortunately, we have all the "true truth" about demons we will ever need in God's Word. Jesus was clear that his mission involved encroaching on the territory and the spheres of influence Satan had developed over the centuries. The true King coming into the world would ultimately result in the complete overthrow of the false king. It's no wonder that evil spirits knew who Jesus was and were afraid of him. His work of salvation included breaking the power of evil in the lives of those being saved.

In chapter eight of Matthew's Gospel we see the fascinating story of a man being delivered from a whole community of demons. Jesus happened to be in Gentile territory, "the region of the Gadarenes" or Gerasenes, when he encountered two mad men. They were so crazy they had been kicked out of their village and were living in the cemetery. Their behavior was so violent the locals were afraid of even walking by those tombs.

But Jesus was not afraid. So, when he walked by, he was recognized by all those demons. Jesus had a reputation in hell. "What do you want with us, Son of God?" (8:29). It's nice that these evil spirits acknowledged Jesus for who he really was. On the other hand, Jesus did not want or need their testimony about him. "Have you come here to torture us before the appointed time?" These demons knew that the coming of the King into the world put an expiration date on the kingdom of darkness and they would be out of a job. I would imagine taking up residence inside of a human being was preferable to hell.

In fact, they preferred residing in pigs than in hell! "If you drive us out, send us into the herd of pigs." That's desperate!

I love how Jesus dealt with the company of demons. He had no magic formulas or talismans. The King's word was final. All the King's authority was contained in the command, **Go**! (8:32). Just one word. And when Jesus spoke the word, the evil spirits had no choice. "So they came out and went into the pigs." Unfortunately, they hadn't counted on the pigs going crazy and rushing down into the lake where they drowned. Their scheme to escape hell didn't work as planned.

As Savior, Jesus didn't just earn salvation in order to make it available to believers. Jesus put all his authority into his work of salvation. He came to command deliverance. And he came to demand healing.

The Command of Healing

There are series of wonderful healing stories in Matthew 8 and 9, the authoritative words of Jesus accomplishing authoritative works. It starts with the healing of a man with leprosy. According to the Old Testament law, a person with leprosy was fundamentally "unclean," so much so, they were required to announce their uncleanness wherever they went. Can you imagine walking around with a sign on your chest that reads, "Unclean"? The real problem with the label of "unclean" was the belief that anyone who came into contact, even casual or accidental contact, with someone who was ruled to be unclean meant that their uncleanness rubbed off. If you accidentally touched a leper, you became unclean, forbidden to touch anyone else. It resulted in a lifestyle of rejection. Talk about low self-esteem!

It's no wonder this man approached Jesus tentatively. "Lord, if you are willing" (8:2). Jesus was a well-known Rabbi. This man acknowledged Jesus as Lord. Certainly, he would not be willing to run the risk of uncleanness by touching this man. On the other hand, the one with leprosy believed in the authority and ability of Jesus to heal someone of their disease, even this horrible disease. "...you can make me clean." In fact, Jesus could have healed this man with a word. Instead, "Jesus reached out his hand and touched the man." It didn't matter that this touch would make Jesus unclean in the eyes of the priests and Pharisees. Jesus was on a mission, and that mission was not to be limited by religious tradition.

"I am willing." It was in the heart of Jesus to heal this man. All that was needed was the pronouncement of an authoritative word. "**Be clean**." This word resulted in an immediate miracle of healing and this man was cleansed of his leprosy. Just one word was required – the authoritative command of healing.

Jesus also recognized the man's need to function within his religious context so he instructed him to show himself to the priest so he could obtain an official pronouncement of the fact that he was now "clean" and could function again within his community. Jesus used his authority to command the man, "**See** that you don't tell anyone." Instead, Jesus wanted the man to go straight to the priest. "But **go**, show yourself to the priest and **offer** the gift Moses commanded, as a testimony to them" (8:4). The witness Jesus was calling for was to be an official one given to the religious leaders of the day, a sure sign of his authority and mission.

ᙢ

The story of Jesus healing the paralyzed man in chapter 9 painted another beautiful picture of the authority of Jesus to command healing. This man was carried by his friends to Jesus, obviously expecting a miracle of healing. They may have received more than they came for.

The account in the Gospel of Mark (that often adds details to the narratives) indicated that these men were not able to get to Jesus, so they dug a hole in the roof and lowered their friend down in front of Jesus (2:1-12). They had a desperate kind of faith.

When Jesus saw the paralyzed man, his first words were a command, perhaps a surprise to the man and his friends as well as an offense to some of the teachers of the law who were present. "**Take heart**." Be encouraged. Be hopeful again. "Your sins are forgiven" (9:2). Evidently Jesus discerned a root issue in this man, resulting in the symptom of paralysis. Jesus also wanted to establish the true nature of his mission to provide salvation. When the teachers accused Jesus of blasphemy, Jesus asked them a question. "Which is easier: to say, 'Your sins are forgiven,' or to say, '**Get up** and walk?'" Jesus was not just a miracle worker, a healer, and a deliverer. Jesus was the Savior. "I want you to know that the Son of Man has authority on earth to forgive sins" (9:6). So, Jesus gave the command to heal. "**Get up**, take your mat and **go**" (9:6).

This situation afforded an opportunity to demonstrate the Savior's authority. The kind of healing/salvation Jesus came to offer was certainly relevant to the repair of mortal human bodies. Even more important, Jesus came to save people from their sins and to heal the consequences of their sins. "Get up, **take up** your mat and **go** home" (9:6). Jesus was the Savior, the Deliverer, the Healer and Restorer, with authority to forgive sins, and to heal the human soul, as well as the human body.

Shortly after, Jesus was confronted by a leader of the local synagogue with a request to raise his daughter from the dead. It took extraordinary faith on the part of this father to believe Jesus could not only restore a diseased body to health, he could also return life to a dead body. As with the story of the leprous man, Jesus well knew that touching a dead body would result in his ceremonial uncleanness. It seemed like an outrageous request, but "Jesus got up and went with him" (9:19).

The first thing Jesus had to do was cancel the wake with a command to the official mourners to "**Go away**" (9:24). Such mourning would not be needed. From Jesus's perspective, "The girl is not dead." Another shocking statement. Jesus not only had authority to heal and forgive, Jesus also had authority over death. "He went in and took the girl by the hand, and she got up." An authoritative touch and a victory over death. The Savior and Life-Giver had come!

Later in chapter 9, Jesus was accosted by two blind men. (Healing the blind was a prophesied Messianic sign (Isaiah 35:5.) These men approached Jesus in an interesting and important way. "Have mercy on us, Son of David" (9:27). They didn't specifically ask for healing but rather, for mercy. They understood their unworthiness to receive any blessing and their absolute dependence on God's mercy. They also confessed that Jesus was the promised Messiah, the greater Son of David.

Jesus brought these men indoors and questioned their faith. "Do you believe that I am able to do this?" Did they really believe that Jesus was the promised Messiah working Messianic miracles? Their response was telling. "Yes, Lord." For whatever reason they had great confidence and trust in this Rabbi from Galilee. They also confessed that Jesus was more than the Jewish Messiah. He was the Lord. They owed him their loyalty as well as their trust.

Jesus then reached out and touched their eyes. Once again, Jesus healed with an authoritative word. "According to your faith **let it be done**" (9:29). Their faith had intersected with the authority of Jesus, resulting in a restoration of their sight. While it is true that Jesus has all authority, whether we believe it or not, when our personal faith and trust meet the absolute authority of Jesus, heaven intersects with earth and something supernatural happens.

Jesus' command of healing was effective in bringing healing to these men. "According to your faith **let it be done**." These men had to believe in the authority of Jesus as well as his power to heal. Yes, it is possible for Jesus to bring healing to a person who has little (or no) faith. It's also possible to accept the authority of Jesus and to believe he is able to heal without actually receiving healing. But when the authoritative word of Jesus meets a believing, trusting heart, great things will happen.

After healing them, Jesus gave these two men a command. "**See** that no one **knows** about this" (9:30). Later in his Gospel, Matthew quoted Isaiah 42:1-4 for an explanation (12:17-21). Contrary to the normal human tendency to promote oneself, the Messiah was to operate in relative obscurity, not crying out to be noticed on the street. Jesus was not going to promote himself or his work. He was on a mission from the Father, a sacred charge that would only be compromised by loud boasts. Jesus chose a gentle approach to his work, not wanting to break a bruised reed or snuff out a smoldering wick. Participation in his mission would require a heart response from his yoked ones, not just loud public declarations.

Unfortunately, these men didn't agree with this Messianic strategy. "But they went out and spread the news about him all over that region." They may have been motivated by a pure love for Jesus and a desire to honor him. It's also possible that there was a note of pride in their disobedience to the command of Jesus.

Words and Works

Jesus made a clear connection between his words and his works. It was not just that his full authority was behind both; somehow the two were intimately linked. One of the most interesting accounts of this link is found in John's Gospel.

In Jesus' "Upper Room Discourse" he made this statement: "The words I say to you I do not speak on my own authority. Rather, it is the Father, living in me, who is doing his work" (John 14:10). The Father working in and through Jesus was resulting in certain words. And those words, when spoken authoritatively, were resulting in certain works. The works of Jesus were evidence that his words were true (verse 11). Both were a demonstration of the authority of Jesus in carrying out the mission of the Father.

I suppose that would just be interesting if not for the next statement Jesus made. "Very truly I tell you, whoever believes in me will do the works I have been doing, and they will do even greater things than these, because I am going to the Father" (verse 12). Jesus was saying that his apprentices, those who would carry on his mission on the earth, would demonstrate his power in the same way, with words and works. And because the Holy Spirit would be guiding and empowering millions of them, the range of those words and works would be greatly extended.

For that reason, seeing how Jesus ministered words and works becomes even more important for today's Kingdom representatives.

Jesus was attending a synagogue one Sabbath when he saw a man with a crippled hand. Jesus knew that the synagogue rulers would object to his healing this man on the Sabbath. So, Jesus began by engaging them in a discussion about what was and was not "legal" to do on the Sabbath day. The descriptions in the Old Testament were fairly general, so the teachers of the law had added a long list of specific Sabbath prohibitions. Jesus asked, "Is it lawful to heal on the Sabbath?" (12:10). Since the synagogue leaders evidently didn't answer his question, Jesus expanded his question. He reasoned that since it was not against their tradition to lift a sheep out of a pit it had fallen into on a Sabbath, and because a person is more valuable than a sheep, healing a person, lifting a person out of their broken condition must be considered legal as well.

After that, Jesus simply spoke an authoritative command. "**Stretch out** your hand" (12:13).   And the word of Jesus, the command to heal, resulted in a supernatural work. "So he stretched it out and it was completely restored, just as sound as the other." The word and the work of Jesus resulted in the complete restoration of this man's hand. The Father was working in Jesus, and when Jesus heard the Father speak a word, he declared that word, and it resulted in a wonderful work of healing.

The Fruit of Discipleship

You would think that those witnessing the words and works of Jesus would glorify the Father as a result. The mission of God was being carried out in an authoritative way. The King had come. The Kingdom of God was being established in earth as it was in heaven.

Instead, the Pharisees claimed that Jesus was speaking and working by the power of Beelzebub, the devil! Jesus reasoned that if the devil was casting out devils, it would result in the fall of his false kingdom. While it made perfect sense, I don't know that it convinced those religious leaders. After all, they weren't so much attempting a reasoned theological argument; they just hated Jesus and were going to say and do whatever they felt would oppose him and (hopefully) offset his good influence.

Jesus was very clear about the situation. "Whoever is not with me is against me" (12:30). After all, Jesus had clearly predicted that his mission would have the effect of dividing people's loyalties. In the end, there were only two camps: those who were with Jesus, and those who were against him.

That had obvious significance for the apprentices of Jesus. They were called to a personal loyalty to the King. They were called to share with Jesus in the mission of God on the earth in every generation. Their participation in that mission would include the Father's words and works continuing through them in greater ways.

But they would also experience opposition. They would experience tribulation. Those opposed to Jesus would be opposed to his apprentices, if they were faithfully living the yoked life.

In the end, both those who were with Jesus and those who opposed Jesus would be known by their fruit. They would be known by the quality of their words and works. The followers of Jesus would be known for the fruit of salvation, deliverance, and healing. Those opposed to Jesus would be known for the fruit of blasphemy, speaking against the Spirit of God and the Son of God.

For that reason, Jesus concluded with an authoritative summary. "**Make** a tree good and its fruit will be good, or **make** a tree bad and its fruit will be bad, for a tree is recognized by its fruit" (12:33). Just take some time to observe the fruit of a person's life. Listen to their words and the effects of their words long enough and you will discover where they stand in the mission of God.

The apprentices of Jesus, those committed to a yoked life, will have the privilege of bearing Kingdom fruit, abundant fruit, fruit that will remain, because it will have eternal significance. And yes, there will be a price to pay, but a price well worth it in the end. Those under the yoke of the Master will have the privilege of hearing and speaking his words of salvation, deliverance, and healing, and will see the powerful works of God as a result. What an awesome privilege!

7 SERMON ON THE KINGDOM

The sermon in the thirteenth chapter of Matthew's Gospel is very unique in that it is made up entirely of parables, and in some cases, private interpretations of parables. Ancient parables were clever stories, told with a single point. They were told in such a way as to capture the imagination of a listener, drawing them into the plot of the story. At the end, the listener was faced with a surprise ending, causing him to reconsider his personal perspectives and values. It was a very creative figure of speech, and Jesus was the master of the parable!

How Badly Do You Want to Hear?

Jesus didn't always teach with parables, and when he did, it was for a very important and strategic reason. Some have said that the Kingdom of Heaven/God was the primary theme of Jesus' teaching, so why communicate so much of that teaching in the form of these creative, perspective-changing stories?

In fact, the disciples asked Jesus that very question. "Why do you speak to the people in parables?" (13:10). Jesus responded (appropriately) with a somewhat cryptic answer. "Because the knowledge of the secrets of the Kingdom of heaven has been given to you, but not to them" (13:11). Wasn't the teaching ministry of Jesus public? Didn't the people acknowledge Jesus to be an important Rabbi? Why take all the time to teach the crowds if he just wanted to keep them in the dark?

Throughout the ministry of Jesus, we see at least two groups of followers. There is no question that a large number of people followed Jesus and listened to his teaching. They also occasionally ate his food. They had a variety of motives for following Jesus other than personal faith and commitment.

And then there were the disciples. While twelve of them were appointed to be "apostles," the larger group had a least 70 in it. (It seems similar to the 12 sons of Jacob and his larger, extended family of 70.) They didn't just follow Jesus around. They had come under the Rabbinic "yoke" of Jesus. They were committed to learning both his words and his life. So, while Jesus had a public ministry, he also had an even more important private ministry to his disciples.

Those with a clear commitment to learning and following retained more of his teaching, digested and applied more of his teaching, and therefore were taught more by Jesus. "Whoever has will be given more, and they will have an abundance" (13:12).

On the other hand, those who were just following Jesus around for the sake of personal benefit, hoping for free health care and meals, although listening, were really not retaining or digesting anything. In reality, they hadn't really received anything. And, "Whoever does not have, even what they have will be taken from them" (13:12). (This saying of Jesus is repeated in Matthew 25:29; Mark 4:25; Luke 8:18; and Luke 19:26.)

Jesus then quoted the words God spoke to Isaiah when giving him his prophetic assignment (Isaiah 6:9-10). "Though seeing, they do not see; though hearing, they do not hear or understand." I've often wondered whether or not Isaiah might have wanted to back out of his calling at that point. "I'm going to put my words in your mouth, Isaiah, but they won't listen to you." So, what's the point!

Some in Isaiah's audience, and in Jesus' audience, would have hearts so hard, they would effectively be blind and deaf. They wouldn't listen because they were unable to listen. However, that was not true for everyone.

"But blessed are your eyes because they see, and your ears because they hear" (13:16). Because of their sincere, heartfelt commitment, the disciples of Jesus were in a position to really hear and understand the teachings of Jesus.

"This is why I speak to them in parables" (13:13). Jesus used very creative teaching stories as a means to see who really wanted to hear his words. Those who really wanted to hear and understand the words of Jesus would seek him out and ask for an explanation. The rest would go their way, happy to have simply heard sounds coming of out the mouth of Jesus, wondering when he would be available for more healings or serve the next meal. A special kind of hearing was required in order to really understand the meaning of the parables of the Kingdom.

Listen and Understand

Jesus gave three commands in the Sermon on the Kingdom, a command that appears three other times in Matthew's Gospel. In fact, it is a command frequently found throughout the New Testament and especially in the "Letters to the Seven

Churches of Asia" in the book of Revelation.

"Whoever has ears, **let them hear**" (13:9, 18, 43). It's no surprise that Jesus would emphasize this command in the context of a teaching made up entirely of parables.

Any parent of a teenager (or wife of an older husband) understands the phenomenon of "selective hearing." Granted, as our hearing gets naturally dull with age at least we have somewhat of an excuse. But for the most part, people hear what they want to hear. And they interpret what they hear the way they want to interpret it. Just speaking loud enough will not guarantee that actual "hearing" is taking place. What is called for is a certain kind of hearing with ears positioned in a certain kind of way.

The word used in these passages (Greek *akouo*) refers to a certain quality of hearing (similar to the Hebrew *shema* in the Old Testament). It describes the kind of hearing that takes place when the hearer has a prior commitment to obeying whatever is heard. It is an active hearing, an interactive hearing. It simply means hearing and obeying. It's interesting that the Greek word for "obey" (Greek *hupakouo*) is a compound form of this word, meaning "to hear under," or to hear as a disciple sitting at the feet of the Master, under the authority of the Master.

The hearing or listening Jesus was referring to is the exact opposite of selective hearing. It is an intensive, focused listening with a passionate desire to understand what is said and a clear commitment to put it into practice.

When Jesus told the initial parable, he ended it by saying, "Whoever has ears, **let them hear**" (13:9). Before Jesus explained the meaning of that parable he commanded the disciples, "**Listen** then to what the parable of the sower means" (13:18). Again, after explaining the meaning of the parable of the weeds, Jesus gave the same command: "Whoever has ears, **let them hear**" (13:43).

Obviously, this quality of hearing requires a certain kind of ears. Jesus had just quoted from the prophet Isaiah a word the Lord had spoken to Isaiah's generation: "You will be ever hearing but never understanding. For this people's heart has become callous" (13:14-15). Clearly, dull hearing is another way of describing a hard heart.

It's possible to become increasingly insensitive to the Lord and to the word of the Lord. It seems to be a natural tendency over time, but it's also possible to simply refuse to hear. And the refusal to hear results in an increasing inability to hear.

Ears that can hear are attentive, mindful ears (or as my wife would say, "a hearing heart"). They are open to hearing whatever the Master might have to say. In fact, they crave any opportunity to hear a word from the Lord. Those are the ears that are willing and ready to hear.

Earlier in Matthew's Gospel, Jesus had been speaking to the crowds about John the Baptist. Jesus placed John in the flow of redemption history, noting that he was the greatest prophet to ever be born, that he was the last of the old prophets, commissioned to prepare the way for the Messiah and the Messianic Kingdom. (Jesus also pointed out the "least in the kingdom of heaven" is greater than John.) Jesus went so far as to say that John was "the Elijah who was to come." A very mysterious statement, a statement Jesus didn't elaborate on. Instead, Jesus gave a familiar command: "Whoever has ears, **let them hear**" (11:15). Those who really wanted to hear, those who were ready to hear, would come to understand the meaning of Jesus' words.

Later in the ministry of Jesus he was teaching another series of parables. Before teaching the parable of the tenants Jesus commanded the listeners, "**Listen** to another parable" (21:33). Jesus understood that not everyone in the crowd would actually be listening to the parable, let alone curious about what it might mean. So, while Jesus taught publicly for everyone in the crowd, in the end his words were intended for those "with ears to hear."

In Matthew 15, Jesus was having a very important conversation with the Pharisees and teachers of the law. They wanted to know why the disciples of Jesus did not wash their hands before eating. (My mother would want to know the same thing.) They had specific rules about "the tradition of the elders." So, Jesus called attention to the tendency of these religious leaders to use their traditions to break very serious elements of the law, including, "Honor your father and mother." Jesus once again quoted Isaiah (29:13) as a criticism of this legalistic approach to morality.

Obviously, the surrounding crowd was listening to this exchange. At the end of it, Jesus turned to the crowd and gave them the command we've heard so many times. "**Listen** (Greek *akouo*)." Jesus was trying to make a very important point about the way God viewed specific laws, and they needed to really pay attention to the point he was making. It was a vitally important principle, and they would be well-served if they gave themselves to attentively, actively hearing.

Jesus then added a second, very important command. **"Listen** and **understand"** (15:10) – another key word used often by Jesus. To "understand" (Greek *suniemi*) basically means to set or to bring together. It means to put it together, to connect the dots, to gain insight in connection to an idea or principle. It means to gain understanding with regard to something in its context. Jesus was not just calling for a superficial grasp of the meaning of his words. Jesus was calling for an in-depth understanding of the essence and the significance of what he was saying. Only those who had ears prepared to actively hear would be able to do so.

It's no wonder Jesus repeated this command in the Sermon on the Kingdom. By definition, parables were used almost as a test to see who was seriously committed to hearing and understanding the message of those parables. Who would take the time to explore the deeper implications of his teaching. After all, Jesus was teaching them about the secrets of the kingdom of heaven.

Secrets of the Kingdom of Heaven

Jesus was using parables to teach about the kingdom of heaven in order to find out who really wanted to hear and understand. Some would say that the "kingdom," either of heaven or of God (who is ruling in heaven) is the central theme of the teaching of Jesus. If so, then seeking to understand the "secrets of the kingdom" is of paramount importance.

To be simple about it, the "kingdom of God" is the domain of the King. It is everywhere the King is ruling. It is the entire sphere of God's ruling authority. The kingdom of God is the complete influence of God – the purpose and the character of God – wherever God is ruling as King.

Jesus came declaring two primary messages: (1) he himself was the King, the ruler of God's Kingdom, and (2) he had come with the mission of extending the rule of God from heaven to the earth. That mission began with the coming of King Jesus into the world and will culminate when every other kingdom has been replaced by God's Kingdom. "The kingdom of the world has become the kingdom of our Lord and of his Messiah, and he will reign for ever and ever" (Revelation 11:15). That is the essence of the Good News Jesus proclaimed. "I am making everything new" (Revelation 21:5).

The disciples of Jesus were ready to hear whatever Jesus had to say about his Kingdom. They may not have fully understood it, and they may have thought he was referring to his Davidic reign over a reconstituted nation of Israel, but in the end, they would faithfully spread the Good News of the Reign of God throughout the world.

The Sermon on the Kingdom was first of all addressed to the crowd. However, at two different times Jesus shared private words of explanation with his disciples (13:10-23, 36-43). The sermon had two sets of four parables each (vv. 3-33 and 44-52), the first four addressed to the crowd and the last four addressed to the disciples.

The Parable of the Soils (13:3-9). Although this parable addresses "the secrets of the kingdom" (v. 11) and "the message about the kingdom" (v. 19), it primarily concerns the need to have listening ears and an obedient heart in order to really understand and live out that message. The teaching ministry of Jesus, and the future teaching mission of the disciples, planted seeds in the hearts and minds of the hearers. However, what happened to that seed depended on the condition of the ears, the hearts of those who were listening.

Jesus used a farming story to describe various heart conditions. The average field in Israel had a variety of soils on it, as evidenced by the pattern of germination and growth of crops coming from the seed. The same kind of seeds were sown everywhere, and every part of the field received the same amount of rain and sunshine. But not every part of the field yielded the same crop.

There were many walking paths in and around those ancient, unfenced fields. The soil on those paths was beaten down and hardened by the trampling of many feet over time. Seed that fell on those paths stayed on the surface, ready for the birds to easily feed on them.

Some parts of the field had underlying bedrock close to the surface. The soil was good but shallow. When seed fell on these rocky places, because the soil was shallow it heated up more quickly and the seeds sprouted quickly. However, because the plants' roots didn't have room to grow, they were quickly scorched in the hot sun and died.

There were patches of thorn bushes around the perimeter of the field. The scattering of seed resulted in some seed falling among these bushes. However, the much larger bushes soon choked out the young plants and they were never able to mature and bear fruit.

However, much of the soil was good, fertile ground, plowed and ready to receive the seed. Depending on the various levels of fertility, a crop grew from the planted seeds. There were various levels of yield for those crops, but every place with good soil bore an abundant crop.

"Whoever has ears, **let them hear**" (13:9).

After an explanation of why parables were being used in this sermon (13:10-17), Jesus took the time to provide his disciples with an explanation of the Parable of the Soils (13:18-23), beginning with the command, "**Listen** then." The meaning of this first parable has to do with the quality of one's hearing and the condition of one's heart. The seed is "the message of the kingdom."

Some people's hearts are hardened, like the path in the field. The falling of the seed has no effect on their heart at all, and the evil one quickly snatches the seed away as if it had never been sown. It's difficult to accept, but some hearts are so hard, no amount of seed or the watering of that seed will germinate in their lives.

Some receive the message in a shallow, thoughtless way. While they exhibit an initial response of enthusiasm and even initial growth, the lack of depth in the soil results in a lack of roots. That becomes evident when "the word is tried" with any kind of trouble. It doesn't take much for the shallow soil to be "scandalized," the initial enthusiasm quickly disappears, and the early faith lost. A shallow heart is the most disappointing of all to us, since there was such an immediate embracing of the word and a quick responsiveness, only to turn back at the first sign of trouble.

Some receive the message but have too many concerns and commitments to allow the seed to grow, mature, and bear fruit. "The worries of this life and the deceitfulness of wealth," the pleasure made possible by wealth, choke the seed and keep it from being fruitful. These hearers are too busy, too distracted, to bring forth the fruit that would have resulted from the message of the Kingdom. It's a challenge for every Jesus follower to keep the thorny distractions of life removed so that the seed of God's Word can prevail and not be choked out.

Other seed falls on good, prepared soil, ears that are ready to hear and hearts that are ready to respond in obedience. They are ready to both hear and understand the message. They take it to heart and inwardly digest its meaning and application to their lives. As a result, "they produce a crop." They bear the fruit of the kingdom, in their lives and in the lives of others. The yield may be 100 times, 60 times, or 30 times what was originally sown, but every place where there is good soil yields a good crop.

In some ways, this description of levels of fruitfulness in the good soil reminds me of the words of Jesus in a later parable. When teaching "the Parable of the Bags of Gold" (chapter 25) Jesus described the distribution of treasure as five bags, two bags and one bag, "each according to his ability." While we Americans may want to think that every human being has the same level of potential, Jesus taught that, while every person has a measure of faith, God has designed different levels of potential fruitfulness resulting in different levels of harvest. However, in the end, everyone is judged equally according to their level of faithfulness.

I remember teaching on this parable many years ago. It was a Bible study aimed at young adults who were all excited to learn about Jesus, his words, and his ways. It was a season of revival. After teaching as I did above, one of the young people asked, "Is there any hope for those with hard, superficial or distracted hearts?" I thought it was a very good and important question. My response occurred to me at that moment. "Yes, if those patches of the field were to be plowed under, their potential fruitfulness could be increased."

"Break up your unplowed ground; for it is time to seek the Lord" (Hosea 10:12).

The Parable of the Weeds (13:24-30). The next six parables all begin with the statement, "the kingdom of heaven is like." (The eighth and final parable refers to "a disciple in the kingdom of heaven.") Clearly the theme is the true nature of God's Kingdom where Jesus rules as the King. This parable paints a picture of the initial sowing of seed in the field and anticipates the eventual harvesting of the seed at the end of the year. "The owner" of the field plants good seed in good soil, anticipating a good harvest. During the interval, "his enemy" sowed weeds in the field. These particular weeds were known as "darnel," a plant very much like wheat. In fact, the young wheat and darnel plants look almost identical. Only after growing for a while can their difference be recognized. There's just one problem. As darnel grows, its roots wrap around the roots of the wheat. So, if a farmer tries to pull the darnel up, they run the risking of pulling the wheat out of the ground as well.

In the parable, Jesus had the servants of the owner ask about pulling the weeds up immediately. Knowing the condition of their roots the owner decided to wait until the harvest to deal with the weeds. At the end of the season, the owner would instruct the servants to "collect the weeds and tie them in bundles to be burned; then gather the wheat and bring it into my barn."

Later in the day Jesus and his disciples left the crowd and went into a house for the evening. In that more private setting, the disciples asked Jesus for an explanation of the Parable of the Weeds (13:36-43). Jesus then gave a very detailed interpretation of the unique parable.

- "The one who sowed the good seed is the Son of Man."
- "The field is the world."
- "The good seed stands for the people of the kingdom."
- "The weeds are the people of the evil one."
- "The enemy who sows them is the devil."
- "The harvest is the end of the age."
- "The harvesters are angels."

This parable of the Kingdom is unique in that it paints a picture of the end of the age. It's not about the average day in the future mission of the disciples. It addresses the big picture of the growth of God's Kingdom community in the real world. It doesn't paint a utopian picture of the community. In fact, it is very clear that there will be "the people of the evil one" always present in the community, looking at first like "the people of the kingdom," but the difference becoming evident over time.

Zeal for the transformative potential of God's Kingdom will cause some to want to pull out those weeds prematurely. After all, "the mixed multitude" can be discouraging, and always a challenging hindrance to the full manifestation of God's glory through God's people. However, Jesus stated that the good seeds, the people of the Kingdom, were being sown in "the world." The mission is the world, and the goal is a harvest. We would like the goal to be some kind of theocratic dominion in the midst of the world. But that is not the mission. The new heavens and the new earth are yet to come.

At the end, there will be a final harvest. Only then will "the weeds be pulled up and burned." At the end, all the weeds will be weeded "out of his kingdom." And the weeds are not just the people of the evil one. They are also "everything that causes sin." Sin and all of its destructive consequences will be extracted from the world as a result of the final coming of God's Kingdom. Only then will "the righteous...shine like the sun in the kingdom of their father." The Kingdom of God in all its glory will be brilliant and glorious with no corruption or imperfection in it.

That promised day is coming but has not yet come. The coming of Jesus, his sowing the people of the Kingdom into the world, started a grand process that will end in the reign of God's Kingdom righteousness, for ever and ever. A final harvest will come. In the meantime, sowing seed and harvesting wheat is the mission of

God's Kingdom representatives, until Jesus comes again.

"Whoever has ears, **let them hear**."

The Parable of the Mustard Seed (13:31-32). Jesus taught a third parable to the crowd, this one very short. "The kingdom of heaven is like a mustard seed, which a man took and planted in his field." Famously, the mustard seed was the smallest seed known in the land of Israel. In fact, it was barely visible in the hand. Mustard plants were obviously used as a source of various kinds of mustard. I'm sure there were other important plants in a garden there. However, there was something unique about this plant.

Although its seed started out as the smallest seed possible, the plant grew to 9 or 10 feet tall in just one year, the largest plant in the garden. In fact, it was so large, birds were actually found to make their nests on the plant. "Though it is the smallest of all seeds, yet when it grows, it is the largest of garden plants, and becomes a tree, so that the birds come and perch in its branches."

It's almost as though Jesus were saying that, although evidence of the Kingdom was starting out very small, almost imperceptible, very quickly it would become the largest plant on earth. The full-grown plant would be the host for birds of all kinds, birds from every tribe on earth, finding a home in its branches.

The Parable of the Yeast (13:33). A fourth parable was then taught to the crowd, this last one also very short. "The kingdom of heaven is like yeast." Yeast is actually a fungus, but it has an amazing effect in a lump of dough. It not only causes it to rise, it also adds a pleasant flavor. The effect of the yeast is internal, where you can't see it. Yeast effects change and growth from the inside out (as opposed to salt or light).

A very small amount of yeast can have an effect on a very large amount of dough. "The kingdom of heaven is like yeast that a woman took and mixed into about sixty pounds of flour until it worked all through the dough." The text refers to "three measures of flour," that is about 50 to 60 pounds of flour, enough to feed a banquet of 100-150 people. In other words, it was a lot of flour! Just a small amount of yeast, when it mixes with the surrounding flour, can have such a pervasive effect it could permeate an entire village.

The internal, even hidden presence of the Kingdom of God, has the power to spread invisibly until the entire surrounding area has been affected. The visible influence of the Kingdom as salt and light is powerful and vitally important, but the invisible influence of the Kingdom as leaven must also be reckoned with. While it's true that each one can and perhaps should demonstrate all three kinds of influence through their lives, I wonder whether or not God calls and equips some citizens of the Kingdom as salt, some as light, and some as leaven.

Matthew then quoted Psalm 78:2 to once again emphasis the use of parables in the teaching ministry of Jesus. "Jesus spoke all these things to the crowd in parables; he did not say anything to them without using a parable" (13:34).

The Parable of the Hidden Treasure (13:44). The last four parables were taught in private by Jesus to his disciples. Having given them a full explanation of the Parable of the Weeds, to bring greater clarity, Jesus revisited his teaching about the secrets of the Kingdom with some additional analogies. "The kingdom of heaven is like treasure hidden in a field." The Kingdom of heaven is like buried treasure, hidden from the surrounding world. Think of the passion of treasure hunters, looking for clues as to the hidden location of some treasure horde, rumored to exist but never proven. Imagine their excitement when they finally discover the treasure they have long been searching for.

"When a man found it, he hid it again." Finding a treasure in a field did not give the treasure hunter the right to claim those riches. The treasure belonged to the owner of the field where the treasure had been hidden. Because the treasure hunter placed such a high value on the treasure he had found, he knew he had to find a way to buy the field where it was located. "And then in his joy went and sold all he had and bought that field."

I'll never forget a young man asking me, "What will it cost me to serve the Lord?" Clearly, he did not yet see the value of that treasure. He maybe didn't even see it as a treasure. And so, he wanted to know what it would cost him. In the parable, the treasure hunter was well aware of the value of the treasure. For that reason, he didn't hesitate to sell "all he had." He completely sold out to gain the possibility of owning the treasure.

I suggest some people are not really looking for treasure. It's so easy to just get used to surviving, to just getting along. It's easy to give up any hope of ever finding a treasure. To begin with, there must be a desire, a longing, a thirst for something more, something better, some kind of treasure that will add more value to life. And there is such a treasure. It is the Kingdom of heaven! The one who sees the infinite, eternal worth of full participation in that Kingdom will "then in his joy" gladly sell everything in order to gain that treasure. To the one who has "ears to hear," the Kingdom of God and the message about the Kingdom is priceless, and no sacrifice is too great for attaining it.

By the way, that young man decided that serving the Lord was worth any price he might ever have to pay. He not only chose participation in the Kingdom, he ended up giving his life for it.

The Parable of the Expensive Pearl (13:45). "The kingdom of heaven is like a merchant looking for fine pearls." What about the case of a very successful merchant who is seeking the ultimate find, the ultimate opportunity to sell the best product to the highest bidder? What if this merchant was specifically looking for very fine pearls?

I recently saw a string of fine pearls selling for nearly $100,000. Any merchant would be glad to discover items this valuable. What if he not only found some fine pearls, he actually found the most beautiful, most valuable pearl of all? Recently the most valuable pearl ever found has been valued at $35 million. What would this merchant do if he found that pearl?

"When he found one of great value, he went away and sold everything he had and bought it." As with the treasure hunter, this merchant, seeking "the pearl of great price," gladly liquidated all of his assets, properties and goods, in order to buy that pearl. And he wouldn't buy it in order to resell it. It would buy it in order to treasure it.

Jesus was teaching that the Kingdom of heaven is the most beautiful, most valuable pearl of all. And those who come to see its value will gladly sell everything, leave everything else behind, in order to live in its beauty.

The Parable of the Net (13:47-50). Jesus then taught a parable with a parallel message to the Parable of the Weeds. "The kingdom of heaven is like a net that was let down into the lake and caught all kinds of fish." No doubt the fishermen in the group would be able to identify with this analogy. Those who fished with nets would understand that when you dragged the net in the water, and especially when you dragged the net along the bottom of the lake, there was no telling what you may haul up. All kinds of fish and water creatures, even refuse, would end up in your net. For that reason, net fishing was just the beginning of the process. You had not "harvested" a catch of fish until you ultimately found a way to separate out and save the "good fish."

"When it was full, the fishermen pulled it up on the shore." Notice that these fishermen did not stop fishing until the net was full. It reminds me of something I read in the letter of James. "See how the farmer waits for the land to yield its valuable crop, patiently waiting for the autumn and spring rains" (5:7). The patient farmer is going to wait to bring in the crops until he is absolutely sure that "the full harvest" has come, that the full potential of the field to bear crops has been exhausted. "Be patient, then, brothers and sisters, until the Lord's coming."

But, that day will come. The net will be as full as it can possibly be. "Then they sat down and collected the good fish in baskets, but threw the bad away." All the fish that are suitable for a good use will be collected, separated from the rest, and put together in one special basket.

The King of the Kingdom, the Lord of the harvest, is committed to the entire harvesting process. The Redeemer is committed to redeeming as many as possible, all who are willing. But in the end, the process in human history will run its course. When the net is full, when the full harvest has been accomplished, a final separation will take place in preparation for the culmination of God's eternal Kingdom. "This is how it will be at the end of the age. The angels will come and separate the wicked from the righteous and throw them into the blazing furnace, where there will be weeping and gnashing of teeth."

No wonder "great patience" is advised. The Lord is not in a hurry to end the harvest season. But the end will come.

Bring Out Treasures New and Old

What an amazing way to conclude the parables of the Kingdom. Jesus then asked the disciples, "Have you understood all these things?" And their answer was even more amazing. "Yes." Really?! These are the secrets of the kingdom, a deep understanding of the reign of the King and the process of its coming "on earth as it is in heaven." My answer might have been, "No, but tell me more!"

And so, Jesus ended this wonderful sermon with one last parable, aimed specifically at his disciples and their commitment to a yoked life.

The Parable of the Teacher of the Law (13:52). "Therefore every teacher of the law who has become a disciple in the kingdom of heaven...." A teacher of the Law, a scribe, was an official interpreter of the Torah in Israel. An honored place. However, they had become enforcers of religious tradition instead of expounders of Scripture in a way that would enlighten their listeners. Instead, Jesus had been modeling a new kind of teacher.

"A disciple of the kingdom of heaven" is someone who has been trained as an apprentice of the Rabbi, and not just any Rabbi, but a King. This is a unique kind of teacher, someone who has come under the yoke of the Kingdom of heaven, who has submitted to the authority of the King. This teacher has been discipled in the ways of the Kingdom and knows how to expound its secrets.

"...is like the owner of a house who brings out of his storeroom new treasures as well as old." A Kingdom trained teacher will be like the owner of a great household, a household so large it contains treasure chambers filled with precious treasure. But this master of the house is not just hording treasures. It is his purpose to bring them out, to release them for the benefit of others.

A yoked Kingdom teacher will have access to various kinds of treasure, specifically, "new treasures as well as old." Because he is "a teacher of the law," old treasures will no doubt be the truths, patterns and principles found in the Old Testament, all of which found their fulfillment in the coming of the Messiah. New treasures must be the new realities made possible because the Messiah had come. The new treasures are the precious pearls revealed by King Jesus. A trained, discipled teacher will know how to expound the secrets of the Kingdom from both the Old and the New.

It's no wonder Jesus repeated the command to **"listen"** and to **"understand."** The calling of a disciple who had found a place fully under the yoke of the Master ultimately included the ability to pass on what had been learned. They wouldn't be called to expound their own unique doctrines but rather the teachings of the Kingdom of heaven as understood in the Law and in the teachings of Jesus. A very careful, active, intentional listening was required if they were to faithfully pass on and commit these precious treasures to others.

And that is our calling and our privilege as disciples under the yoke of Jesus!

8 SERMON ON THE CHURCH

The Kingdom of God is "the big picture" of God's rule, the King's Domain. Because God is present everywhere at the same time, God's rule is everywhere at the same time. I'm very thankful God decided to extend God's righteous influence to the world of human beings, to our world. God didn't just design and setup creation and then leave us to figure it out. Everything God has made works best when it exists and functions within the context of the rule of God.

On the other hand, God's Kingdom has always had a Kingdom community. For God's rule to be applicable and practical in our experience, we need to see how it is designed to work in the context of human relationships. While the church is not the Kingdom, the church is God's present Kingdom community, the primary new covenant community. The problem with the church is that there are human beings in it. If there were only elect angels in the church, it would be a much more pleasant experience for all concerned. But there are real, ragged, broken human beings making up God's community. When you think about it, the fact that God has chosen to constitute the Kingdom community this way should inspire us to seek expressions of the rule of God through our fallible human lives and relationships in this thing we call the church.

Children of the Kingdom

Matthew chapter 18 records important teachings of Jesus on the church. The sermon was introduced by a question from the disciples. "Who, then, is the greatest in the kingdom of heaven?" I suppose it is only natural for sin-affected human beings to turn everything into a competition. After all, the essence of sin is self-centeredness and the tendency to attempt to live life independently from God. This kind of self-focus is not only a stumbling block to personal spiritual growth and health, it is also a very serious hindrance to the life and health of the community.

So, Jesus answered their question with a human "object lesson." He called a little child to come forward and placed him in the middle of these self-important disciples. What he then said was so important he introduced his statement with,

"Amen. I say to you," or, "Understand that what I am about to say to you is fundamentally and foundationally true and important."

"Unless you change and become like little children, you will never enter the kingdom of heaven." "Changing" in this statement means to turn around and change direction. In other words, unless you reverse course and think differently about this "greatness" issue, you will never grasp the true meaning and potential for life in the Kingdom.

A little child is certainly not perfect. Anyone who has ever raised a two-year old understands that every human being is "born in sin." However, a little child is not class conscious. A little child does not weigh words and actions by whether or not it will make him look good or be the "greatest." There is a simpler, more innocent approach to life and to relationships. There is a basic kind of humility in a small child's approach to life, always curious, ready to learn, ready to adapt. This characteristic will be an important key to a disciple's ability to live a yoked life and to live it in community with other disciples.

"Greatness" is to be redefined in God's Kingdom. Someone who is willing to humble himself, to take the low position, to be the least, will be now considered "great." This not only has profound significance for individual disciples, it is also a guiding principle for the way disciples relate with each other. "And whoever welcomes one such child in my name welcomes me." This statement uses the same word Paul would later use when he exhorted the believers in Rome to "accept one another," to welcome, receive and embrace one another, including those who seem to have weak faith. (Romans 14 & 15 contain a wonderful extended application of the teaching of Jesus in this passage.)

Citizens of the Kingdom of heaven will be known for receiving and accepting those who are in a low position, a place of humility and vulnerability. In fact, when they accept the "weak" and "lowly," the "little ones" and the "least of these," they will be accepting Christ himself. Jesus identifies himself with all of his followers, but does so in a special way those who have the greatest need and seem to be less significant, less "great," than others.

It is no wonder that in the very next chapter, Jesus would be seen welcoming all of the children brought to him. When the disciples considered this to be beneath the dignity of the Messiah, he rebuked them, and commanded them to "**Let** the little children come to me" (19:14). Further, he commanded the disciples, "**do not hinder** them," do not put anything in front of the children that would confuse or discourage them from seeking a blessing from the Lord. "For the kingdom of heaven belongs to such as these." While he was referring to children, in chapter 18 he was referring to more than children, he was describing the unique relational dynamic of the human Messianic community.

Stumbling Blocks

The personal care Jesus had for "a little child" was extended more generally to "these little ones." Those who have entered the Kingdom of heaven – the ones who have a childlike humility and faith – are those who believe in Jesus. As a community they are viewed by Jesus as little ones, needing care and protection.

There is the real danger of obstacles being put in the way of these little ones, things that could cause them to stumble, that could weaken their faith or cause them to fall into sin. The word used here is *skandalizo* and refers to a stumbling block. (We obviously get our English word "scandalize" for this word.) While the community of Jesus has genuine believers with a genuine humility and faith, it is possible for there to be people and circumstances that would scandalize those "little ones." As the shepherd of the sheep, the King of the Kingdom, and the head of his community, Jesus takes the danger of stumbling blocks very seriously.

In fact, Jesus described a common form of Roman execution – drowning – as a just penalty for anyone who caused a little one to stumble. This was not just a minor issue in the community but a potentially life-and-death issue, both for the one stumbling and the one causing to stumble.

But it's not just a problem of certain members of the community bringing stumbling blocks into the lives of its members. Jesus was clear about the root and source of these stumbling blocks. "Woe to the world!" The original source of the things that cause people to stumble is the world, humanity organized independently from God. Those stumbling blocks may have been introduced by a member, but their source is the world.

"Woe to the person through whom they come!" In the end, individual believers must take responsibility for bringing causes of stumbling into the community, endangering individual little ones and endangering the community as a whole.

To emphasize the seriousness of this problem, Jesus used a saying from the Sermon on the Mount (5:29-30) but in a different context with different applications. In doing so, he repeated four important commands. "If your hand or foot causes you to stumble, **cut** it off and **throw** it away." In this case, the "hand" or "foot" was not something in a person's character that needed to be eliminated but rather someone in the community. "And if your eye causes you to stumble, **gouge** it out and **throw** it away." Some commentators suggest that hands and feet symbolize active members and activities while eyes may refer to the visionary aspects of leadership. In any case, if "the fire of hell" is literally at stake, hard choices will have to be made in order to protect the little ones, those who believe in Jesus.

From the beginning, we see that Jesus' Sermon on the Church is going to make us a bit uncomfortable. Jesus seemed to take his community more seriously than most of us members. While the Gospel is the Good News of God's grace and forgiveness, and while the community is to be inclusive, accepting those who seek to gather, it is also necessary to be honest and discerning about the dangers involved. Some of those dangers present the immediate possibility of stumbling, of falling into sin and falling from faith. In such cases, appropriate steps, even radical steps, will be required to protect the lives and well-being of the sincere followers of Jesus.

But unless you think Jesus was just being unnecessarily harsh, he immediately clarified his concern with a beautiful parable.

Wandering Sheep

The warnings about stumbling blocks come in the context of a passionate concern and care for Jesus' "little ones." See that you do not despise one of these little ones" (18:10). Be careful not to look down on or entertain wrong ideas about a true disciple of Jesus. Avoid scorning or disregarding a sincere member of the faith community as if they were insignificant. In some sort of way, they are actually represented in heaven. Heaven does not disregard them but recognizes their worth in the presence of God.

The Parable of the Wandering Sheep painted a picture of the care Jesus had for his little ones. If one sheep out of a herd of one hundred wandered away, for any reason, a true shepherd would leave the ninety-nine in order to look for the one. And when the shepherd finds the one wanderer, he would rejoice over that one more than over all the other ninety-nine put together! The heart of the shepherd is connected to and committed to all the sheep, and especially those who are vulnerable and need more attention.

"In the same way your Father in heaven is not willing that any of these little ones should perish" (18:14). God values every follower of Jesus and is personally careful and protective of each one individually. The heart of the Father is for the protection and restoration of every sheep.

So, when Jesus addresses the case of a brother who sins, the issue is twofold: (1) Someone in the community is actively placing dangerous stumbling blocks in the path of one or more other member, and (2) while that danger must be honestly addressed, finding a way to restore the guilty member must also be sought. There are no throw-away disciples, including the one causing the stumbling.

What kind of sin might Jesus have had in mind? The word translated "sin" (Greek *harmartia*) is the general word for sin, "missing the mark," falling short of the glory of God. However, in the context, this incident of sin poses an immediate and dire threat to one or more members of the community, if not the community as a whole. It's not just a personal offense but a dangerous stumbling block.

In this situation Jesus spoke an authoritative word, providing several very important commands to his followers. First of all, he commanded them to "**go**" and "**point out**" their sin. The one who had become aware of the situation was to take the initiative and respond actively. The idea of "pointing out" referred to an act that exposed the true nature of something with the goal of bringing conviction, confession, and ultimately repentance. Because God is a God of restoration, this first very important step is to be person-to-person, one person confronting another in private. Confronting the one causing a stumbling block must be done prayerfully, since the hope is for a sincere turning away from whatever has become a danger in the community. The best outcome is for the one who is sinning to listen to the one confronting him, and if they do, "you have won them over," or literally, "you will have gained your brother," you will have succeeded in rescuing your brother and guarding his participation as a member of the community.

But what if he refuses to listen? What if he is not willing to acknowledge the problem and the danger it poses? He might even get angry and claim that this is nothing more than a personal attack. What then?

"Take one or two others along" (18:16). In the end, if some kind of corrective action is to be taken, it cannot be based on the evidence provided by one person alone. To support this second step, Jesus referred to Deuteronomy 19:15. The Mosaic Law was very clear on this subject. Every fact was to be established by at least two or three witnesses. And the accused had the right to answer the claims of these witnesses face-to-face. Anything less was an injustice.

These additional two or three were to be witnesses of the offense, to have personal evidence of the wrong that had brought a serious danger into the community. Most commentators agree that these were likely to be leaders in the community, making the evidence even more convincing. This group of witnesses was to have the same goal as the original confronter: to reason with the offender in a way that would result in a changed attitude and changed behavior. The goal was repentance and restoration.

But what if in the face of all this evidence, what if when being confronted by a group of godly eyewitnesses who were the respected leaders in the community, what if the one posing a serious danger to the church still refused to listen? In fact, he may have felt ganged up on at this point and responded by inventing new justifications for his dangerous words and deeds. What if he dug his heals in and simply refused to acknowledge the problem, let alone turn from it?

In such a tragic case, Jesus gave two more clear commands. This group of leaders was to "**tell**" it to the church. In the end, the entire community needed to be aware of the issue and the need to take protective and redemptive action. And if the offender refused to listen to the pleas of the entire community? "**Let him be** to you like a Gentile or a tax collector." While it may seem harsh, in the Jewish community being taught by Jesus and Matthew, Gentiles and tax collectors were like untouchables in India. In the Old Testament Levitical sense, the one who refused to listen, who refused to repent in any way, was "unclean" and not to be associated with.

He was to be removed from the fellowship, from the network of relationships in the community. In the words of Jesus' earlier teaching, if he was a "hand" or a "foot," he was to be cut off. If he is an "eye," he was to be gouged out. But that was not the end of the story! There was more to come.

By the way, this is serious business! I have heard some believers use this teaching from Jesus as an excuse to confront anyone who offends them. However, the situation being addressed by Jesus was literally a life-and-death matter, an issue that, unless a place of repentance and restoration could be found, would result in serious harm if not destruction to more vulnerable members of the community if not the community as a whole. While my purpose is not to explore the details of church discipline, may I suggest that the fifth chapter of Paul's first letter to the church at Corinth be studied to get a fuller picture of how this might be worked out in an actual local church.

A Messianic Gathering

When Jesus described the third and last step in the confrontation process, he used a unique word. "**Tell** it to the church." Many have pointed out that the word "church" is only found three times in the Gospel of Matthew (two of them in 18:17) and it isn't used at all in the other Gospels. On the other hand, the word "kingdom" is used over 50 times in the Gospel of Matthew (four times in chapter 18) and over 60 times in the other Gospels. Clearly the underlying idea is the Kingdom rule of God in heaven brought to earth by King Jesus.

But every Kingdom has a real-life, flesh-and-blood human community. It is the assignment of that community to express the nature of the Kingdom and to extend its influence in earth. Being human, a Kingdom community is not perfect, but it has a vitally important mission as a representative of the reign of King Jesus, each individual community in its own unique time and place.

Simply put, the church is the human community of King Jesus. The mission of the church is therefore to reflect, in imperfect but important ways, the unique characteristics of a Messianic community in the midst of the world, and to recruit and train apprentices of Jesus everywhere it is found. In other words, the church is the primary instrument of the Kingdom of God in this age. While the Kingdom is the end and goal, the church is the primary means toward that end.

You may have heard that the Greek word translated "church" is *ekklesia*. It literally means "the called-out ones" and referred in classical Greece to how democracy worked. During the time when there was democracy in Greece, every citizen (white, land-owning males) of a Greek city or *polis* was asked to rule on matters that came before the city. When a city meeting was needed, the citizens were "called out" of their homes to meet in a central location. That meeting, that gathering of the citizens, was called the *ekklesia*. (It was not an *ekklesia* while the citizens were still in their homes.)

So, when Matthew quoted Jesus' use of *ekklesia* three times, Jesus was proposing the establishment of an actual, real-life human community that would represent his Kingdom rule and Kingdom mission on the earth, during real times and in real places.

The first and most general (if not foundational) use of *ekklesia* is found in Matthew 16:18. While unpacking the details of that passage goes beyond my purpose here, it is important enough to take a brief look at it, especially since similar language is used in the Sermon on the Church.

While meeting privately with his disciples Jesus asked them to report on what they heard others saying about him. Evidently some speculated that Jesus was John the Baptist come back from the dead, or Elijah come down out of heaven. Others that he might even be Jeremiah or one of the prophets, or at least someone functioning in the same anointing. After all, it had been Moses who had predicted that God would eventually raise up "a prophet like me," understood to be a Messianic prediction.

Finally, Jesus asked his disciples what their view of him was. In response, Peter gave a very clear and accurate confession. "You are the Christ, the Son of the Living God" (16:16). It was such a good statement Peter may have been impressed with his own words! However, Jesus clarified that Peter had not come up with this understanding on his own but that it had been revealed to him "by my Father in heaven."

And then Jesus mentioned his church for the first time. "I will build my church, and the gates of hell will not prevail against it." This is a clear promise from Jesus about his intent, his commitment, to building a concrete human *ekklesia* that would express and extend his Kingdom rule in the earth.

I can't help but notice a couple of important aspects of this Kingdom gathering: (1) It belongs to Jesus, it is his church, not that of any leader or tribe; (2) its mission will be offensive, not defensive, breaking down the gates of hell that will not be able to prevail against it; (3) It is to be built on the cornerstone of Jesus himself (not Peter or Peter's confession); and (4) It is an authoritative community, sharing in the authority of heaven. After all, the mission of the church is to see God's rule and God's will done on earth as it is in heaven.

So, that brings us to Jesus' second use of *ekklesia*. "If they refuse to listen, **tell** it to the church; and if they refuse to listen even to the church, **treat** them as you would a pagan or a tax collector" (18:17). At the very least, the "church" being referred to in this chapter is a concrete gathering of disciples. It involves real people gathering in real places at real times. It involves important covenant relationships and the pastoral involvement of real leaders. In other words, the church is a flesh-and-blood community of human beings.

The statements of Jesus in verses 18-20 then connect directly back to chapter 16. "Truly I tell you." "Amen, I say to you," introducing a very important statement. "Whatever you bind on earth will be bound in heaven, and whatever you loose on earth will be loosed in heaven." These are the same words used by Jesus in 16:19, referring to "the keys of the kingdom of heaven." The church will share in the authority of heaven. However, it's important to notice that the headquarters of the Kingdom is heaven, not the church. In fact, there is a footnote in my Bible at 18:18 pointing out that "will be bound" and "will be loosed" is better translated "will have been bound" and "will have been loosed." The language used by Jesus in both chapter 16 and chapter 18 makes it clear that the authority being used in the church originates in heaven. The church has the authority to "bind" and "loose" on earth as a result of that binding and loosing being first of all declared in heaven.

"Binding" and "loosing" in chapters 16 and 18 connect nicely to the idea of "keys" and can refer to "locking" and "unlocking" as well as "tying up" and "untying." While the immediate context is church discipline, I agree that there are much larger implications. Acting on the word of heaven, the church will have the authority to both discipline and restore a stumbling block-causing member. The mission of the church will also require the direct and consistent authority of heaven clearing out obstacles put before them and setting the captives free. How else will the church be able to prevail against the gates of hell.

Jesus then followed up with a very important additional statement, one that makes the reality of the earthly gathering in connection to heaven even clearer. "If two of you on earth agree about anything they ask for, it will be done for them by my Father in heaven" (18:19). When there is agreement, two (or more) of them saying the same thing, about any matter on earth, as a request before the Father, it will be done in heaven. What a powerful statement! It describes the power of agreement, including agreement in corporate prayer. If there is two-way agreement, agreement between two or more members of the church and agreement between those members and heaven, it will be done by the Father. While heaven is taking the initiative, it is up to the church to discern that initiative, to discern the Father's will in heaven, and to agree together as they agree with heaven. Only then will it be done on earth as in heaven. The church has the authority to bring the will of God from heaven to earth! It's no wonder that the foundational prayer is, "Your kingdom come, your will be done, on earth as it is in heaven."

"For where two or three gather in my name, there am I with them" (18:20). Wherever there is a gathering of the *ekklesia* of the King, even if it is only two or three, if they are gathering in the name of Jesus, if they are gathering under the authority of Jesus, representing Jesus in their gathering, then he promises to be in their midst. He will be present among them.

Agreeing together with each other and with heaven, while a powerful, effective, authoritative reality, it is even more personal and intimate. Jesus is the central figure, both in the gathering on earth and with the Father in heaven. In the end, it's not about the church, it's about King Jesus! It is his church representing and agreeing with his Father in heaven. After all, Jesus is King in heaven and on earth, present in and through his Kingdom community.

A Community of Reconciliation

Some may wonder whether or not harsh, judgmental, self-righteous members of the community might use the teaching of Jesus about the rare but needed process of church discipline. What if some people, out of a so-called zeal to "protect" the sheep, end up preaching an exclusive Gospel and operate their gathering as if it were a gated community? Is it possible that someone might forget the overriding theme of forgiveness and reconciliation?

It is evident that the disciples listening to Jesus teach on the church understood that in the end, for the church to represent the nature of God's Kingdom, forgiveness, not discipline, was to be the last word. Granted, concrete forgiveness cannot be granted apart from sincere repentance. But the goal, from first to last, is to create a community of forgiveness and reconciliation.

Peter demonstrated his understanding with a question. "Lord, how many times should I forgive my brother or sister who sins against me? Up to seven times?" (18:21). Peter knew that Jesus was a strong proponent of the "greater righteousness" of the Kingdom. The Rabbis taught that a person could be forgiven for a repeated sin a maximum of three times. In this context, Peter was suggesting that true disciples go so far as to forgive someone up to a maximum of seven times for a repeated sin. In other words, what if a brother keeps introducing a stumbling block, even the same stumbling block, into the community and then repents for having done so? The Rabbis taught a "three-strikes-and-you're-out" policy. Maybe the Messianic community might go so far as to allow seven strikes!

"I tell you, not seven times, but seventy-seven times" (18:22). Frankly, that really seems impossible. I can imagine having difficulty forgiving and reconciling (if church discipline had proved to be necessary) someone three times for the same offense, let alone seven times. So, what is Jesus saying?

In order to count the times when forgiveness has been extended, it will have been necessary to keep a record of offenses. In essence, Jesus was saying that forgiveness is to be the climate, the atmosphere, of the church. "Love...keeps no record of wrongs" (1 Corinthians 13:5).

To emphasize his point Jesus then taught an amazing parable. The Parable of the Unmerciful Servant is another Kingdom parable. "Therefore, the kingdom of heaven is like..." (18:23). The unique nature of God's Kingdom is known for a quality that is indeed humanly impossible. Apart from the supernatural involvement of God's grace and Spirit, this quality is not possible for self-centered, self-focused human beings.

The parable told the story of a king who wanted to settle accounts with his servants, beginning with a particular servant who owed "ten thousand talents." This translation doesn't really do justice to what Jesus was saying. There isn't a word for "ten thousand" in Greek. The word in the text is "myriad," simply the highest number that could be stated. And a "talent" was the highest weight that could be stated. It was the amount of weight a soldier could carry on his back, usually between 75 and 100 pounds. If the weight being carried was in silver, it would have approximated 20 years of wages, and much more if it was in gold. If we take a "myriad" of talents to be ten thousand, it would have amounted to 200,000 years of wages, or over a billion dollars in today's currency. Another way of looking at this huge debt was that it amounted to more than the actual value of the entire Roman province of Israel. An impossible debt! An impressive example of Rabbinic hyperbole!

So, what did the king do? At first, he acknowledged that the only reasonable result of a debt this size was that he and his family be sold into slavery. I looked up what I might have been worth as a slave in the Roman empire (assuming I was much younger) and found out I might have been worth almost two years of wages. So, if the king sold me into slavery, I would have been able to work off the debt in 10,000 years. It's just not possible!

Realizing how impossible this was, the servant begged for mercy. He repented. And the result? The Lord showed mercy to him, "canceled the debt," and let him go. He forgave the impossibly huge debt and "loosed" the servant, setting him free to go. This is the Gospel in a nutshell.

Having been forgiven an almost unlimited debt, how did that servant respond? He went out and found a fellow servant that owed him a debt worth 100 days of wages, and he responded with violence, grabbing and choking the man, demanding the immediate repayment of the debt. When the poor fellow servant begged for mercy, the recently forgiven servant responded by throwing him into debtor's prison. In the Roman Empire, it was illegal to throw someone into debtor's prison for a debt less than that person would have been worth if sold into slavery. The least expensive slave could be sold for as little as the equivalent of 500 days' wages. In other words, it was illegal to throw the poor servant into debtor's prison for the paltry debt of 100 days wages.

Somehow this forgiven servant did not really understand the ideas of repentance and forgiveness. He certainly had not learned to pray, "Forgive us our debts, as we also have forgiven our debtors." He didn't see that forgiveness was a core quality of the Kingdom of heaven, and therefore of the Kingdom community. Forgiveness was to be a guiding principle, governing relationships in the community based on a clear understanding that, because God has forgiven us an unbelievably impossible debt against him, we will be quick to find reason to forgive others when they sin against us.

Of course, when the King and Lord found out what had happened, he called the rich servant back and, with a sharp rebuke, delivered him over to be tortured until his entire debt was paid. "But if you do not forgive others their sins, your Father will not forgive your sins" (6:15).

The conclusion? "This is how my heavenly Father will treat each of you unless you forgive your brother or sister from your heart" (18:35). Even if an offending brother, refusing at first to repent, has been removed from the fellowship of the community, when he comes with sincere repentance, he must be forgiven. The church is a Kingdom community that takes care of its little ones, but as representatives of the King, it is governed by a commitment to forgiveness and reconciliation. It is a place of acceptance and healing. A place of restoration. A community of reconciliation.

So, although not perfect, the church, the King's Kingdom community, strives to model forgiveness, equal care for all, and reconciliation.

9 THE COMMAND TO WATCH AND PRAY

The yoked life is not automatically or mechanically governed by principles and rules. A disciple can never say, "OK, I've got it! I'll take it from here!" A disciple never fully graduates as an apprentice of Jesus, can never say that she or he has fully and perfectly learned how to grasp and keep all the things Jesus has commanded and instructed. The yoked life is a life of relationship, the apprentice under one side of the yoke with the master under the other side.

The Yoked life is a lifestyle of careful attention, mindfulness and discernment. Too much confidence that I have mastered the principles and commandments of my apprenticeship will result in an unfortunate, even a tragic, carelessness. To avoid that possibility Jesus provided several commands to watch and prayer.

Pay Attention

The Pharisees and Sadducees were constantly hanging around, try to trip Jesus up in his words or his actions. In many ways, they represented the opposite of the lifestyle of the Kingdom Jesus came to announce and model. But they were also the religious leaders of first-century Judaism. The Pharisees were the conservative lay leaders in the community who held to a high view of the Scriptures and worked to maintain the traditions of Judaism through the Rabbis and the synagogues. The Sadducees were the priestly class, the official leaders of temple worship. It was hard to disagree with them, and even harder to see how they were misunderstanding and misrepresenting God.

Seeing the danger posed by the religious leaders required a very careful and thoughtful discrimination on the part of the disciples.

More than once, these hypocritical leaders tested Jesus "by asking him to show them a sign from heaven" (16:1). They had witnessed the signs Jesus had already shown in his ministry, the works of the Father that gave witness to the words of the

Father. But they were unable (or unwilling) to see that the works of the Father originated from the throne of the Father in heaven. They couldn't (or wouldn't) see past the normal human tendency to view the supernatural as magic, an ability that when gained could be called on at will. They thought Jesus should be able to simply decide to initiate a miracle, and *voila,* something supernatural would happen.

It reminds me of the time when Israel was traveling through the desert and couldn't find any drinking water. They immediately slipped into grumbling mode, suggesting that it would have been better to remain as slaves in Egypt. Of course, the Lord was gracious and instructed Moses to strike the rock with his staff, and when he did, water was miraculously released for the people to drink. Moses named that place Massah (testing) and Meribah (quarreling). What I find interesting is the way the people tested the Lord. They asked the question, "Is the Lord among us or not?" (Exodus 17:7). When you think about it, that was a really dumb question. They had just experienced the signs and wonders in Egypt, the miraculous passage through the Red Sea, the healing of the waters at Marah, and the provision of manna and quail. All they had to do was look up and see the cloud of God's glory by day and the pillar of fire by night. So why ask such a stupid question?

They were simply trying to manipulate God into doing what they were asking God to do. It would be like a young man asking his girlfriend, "Do you love me or not?" But when you think about, all occult practices and pagan religion, indeed all of "religion," is an attempt to manipulate the gods to bless or to curse, to do whatever we are asking them to do.

The way of God's Kingdom assumed that God was in control, that God's will was to be done on earth as it was being done in heaven, with heaven initiating and earth responding. Jesus was not a magician. Jesus was the Savior of the world, God's Son.

The religious ideas being taught and represented by the Pharisees and Sadducees were an alternative to the Kingdom Jesus was teaching and representing. They were also a subtle trap that needed to be discerned and avoided by the disciples.

For that reason, Jesus gave his disciples a very firm warning and command. "'**Be careful**, Jesus said to them. "'**Be on your guard** against the yeast of the Pharisees and Sadducees" (16:6). The command to **"be on your guard"** (Greek *prosecho*) was often repeated by Jesus. It was a word the ancient Greek writers, especially philosophers, really loved. It meant to turn your mind to something, to give careful heed to something, to pay attention to it. It referred to being alert to – intentionally noticing something. It assumed that an observer really cared for the thing he was alert to, was genuinely concerned about it. And it wasn't just a passive alertness or concern but rather implied that the person was occupied with and devoted to the observation of a thing and the need to take appropriate action after observing it. In other words, it was a very intense focus on a person, thing, or idea, especially one that posed a potential danger.

Anything less than this level of attention would fail to alert the disciples to the dangers involved in the perspectives, values, and teachings of the religious leaders of their day. The nature of that danger was clarified when Jesus referred to it as "yeast." As you'll recall, yeast worked invisibly, internally, in a way that could not be clearly or immediately seen. Nevertheless, yeast had a powerful, thorough, ongoing influence. The only way to avoid the influence of the yeast is to avoid the yeast altogether. So, how is it possible to avoid something you can't see, ideas whose subtle and largely acceptable influence works on the inside? It's simply not possible without a careful, intentional attentiveness.

Jesus made this point even more forcefully by using two commands, a double-barreled commandment. Not only were the disciples to "**be on guard**," they were also to "**be careful**." The command to "be careful" (Greek *horao*) added an emphasis on noticing something, catching sight of it, recognizing and understanding the significance of it. It referred to an active witnessing and personal experiencing of something. In fact, this word was also used to refer to seeing a vision. It also involved a command to take care of something, to "see to it."

When the disciples failed to understand his meaning, Jesus repeated it. "**Be on your guard** against the yeast of the Pharisees and Sadducees" (16:11). This time they understood Jesus to be referring to "the teaching of the Pharisees and Sadducees." Their initial lack of understanding itself demonstrated the need for greater attention to issues and challenges surrounding them every day.

It's possible to go through life somewhat carelessly, not really paying all that much attention to what's going on around us. And it's not just a matter of normal distractions but of a consistent state of mind. How much do we really notice? Do we take the time to discern and reflect on the dynamic elements in our environment, including the ideas being communicated and lived out? Do we really understand that we are living in a world where two kingdoms are in conflict, indeed, are at war, and that constant vigilance is required? It's very easy to just be simple or naïve. There are times and places (and among some groups of people) when I have caught myself admitting, "ignorance is bliss." That may have been a convenient conclusion at the time, but a blissful, ignorant way of life is really very dangerous. The command of

Jesus to "be careful" and to "be on your guard" is vitally important to the yoked life of his apprentices.

Be Alert

A profoundly important story that demonstrates the need for constant spiritual vigilance can be found in the Garden of Gethsemane. Just after the last supper with his disciples and before the upcoming trial and execution of Jesus, he spent three hours in intense, agonizing prayer. He wanted it to be a private time with the Father, but he also felt the need to have three of his disciples close by.

So, Jesus took Peter, James, and John with him and showed them a place to sit while he went some distance further into the garden to pray. We know the story of the wrestling that took place in prayer, the full extent of the redemption about the be accomplished and the trauma involved. Jesus admitted to his friends, "My soul is overwhelmed with sorrow to the point of death" (26:38).

Before going on to pray Jesus gave them two commands. "**Stay** here and **keep watch** with me." Jesus wanted his disciples to share in his moment by staying with him in a place of watchfulness.

Jesus used a very simple but important word to communicate the need to "keep watch" (Greek *gregoreo*). It simply means to stay awake or to keep your eyes open. It means to be watchful or alert. And it's not just a passive alertness but rather the need to be wide awake. In fact, figuratively this word could be used to refer to someone who was truly alive rather than dead ("asleep"). Our idea of continual, consistent vigilance accurately describes the meaning of this word and of the command of Jesus.

Be alert! Keep your eyes open! Don't fall asleep when intense vigilance is required!

Unfortunately, after spending an hour in agonizing prayer and spiritual warfare, Jesus returned to find his friends asleep. It could have been that they had imbibed too much of "the fruit of the earth" during supper, or it was maybe just past their bed time. In any case, the situation called for an unusual amount of alertness. The dangers were great, and the time was at hand. A lack of alertness can result in the loss of an opportunity to share in the purposes of God at that moment.

I've noticed that in life we experience periodic times I think of as "prophetic moments." They are moments when a window in heaven seems to open up, giving us an opportunity to participate in the mission of God in important and even supernatural ways. That window remains open for a fairly short amount of time, so that if we are asleep, not alert to that Kingdom moment, it may just pass us by.

We never know when a Gethsemane moment – or need – may present itself. It is best to stay alert at all times.

Pray

The three hours spent in the Garden of Gethsemane provided one of the very best examples of the need to watch and pray. The instructions and responses of Jesus to his disciples are still relevant to his disciples today.

Jesus began by positioning his three friends to best participate in the coming hours. When he brought them into the Garden, he commanded them to "**Sit** here while I go over there and pray" (26:36). It can be hard to find the balance between hyper-activity and complete passivity. The occasion was the need to support Jesus during his time of prayer. They were to sit – alertly, attentively, ready to respond to whatever need might arrive. They were to sit – acknowledging the authority of their Master, prepared to serve his needs. They were not to be looking for things to do, not pacing around wondering what was happening, not planning what to do in case one of those things actually happened. Nor were they to lie down and sleep. They were to stay awake, focused on the prophetic importance of the moment.

After spending an hour in deep intercession Jesus returned to find the three asleep. While they had failed in the simple assignment to "sit," rather than rebuking them Jesus gave them invaluable instruction, with two words of command. "**Watch**," the word we have already seen, meaning to keep watch and remain alert. However, this time Jesus combined his command with a second one. "**Pray**." There are several words in the Bible translated "pray." This one can refer to earnest intercession. It paints a picture of someone assuming a position of prayer, either kneeling or prostrate on the ground. In other words, Jesus wanted his companions to share in this moment with him. They were not just to occupy space; they were to watch and pray.

Why command these disciples to watch and pray? What was at stake?

Without the vital combination of alertness and prayerfulness, there was a distinct possibility that the disciples would fall into a severe test unprepared. To be asleep when a time of trial and testing comes would result in a tragic failing of that test. And the consequences could be dire and possibly permanent.

Even as disciples, these three – and each of us even now – lived in a contradictory reality. "The spirit is willing," the inner man, passionately committed to the lordship of Jesus, is eager and prepared, ready to serve the Master in any and every situation. Ready to pay the price of that service no matter what it might be. However, the flesh, the fallen mortal aspects of our existence, are weak, are sick, and diseased. All of us experience the constant conflict between our willing spirit and our defective flesh. However, we can choose a commitment to learning how to watch and pray, certainly during trying times, but ultimately even as a lifestyle.

This kind of prayer is more than a rehearsing of our needs before the Lord, although the Lord values that communication. It is more than a set time of worship and supplication, although that discipline makes an important contribution to our overall spiritual health and life. This kind of prayer is even more than intercession. To "watch and pray" is to stay alert in the presence of the Lord, listening attentively, watching for the hand of God, looking for a need that might call for heaven-initiated action. It is a 24/7 humble and submissive readiness to hear and to obey.

This kind of prayer will not only keep us from failing and falling into a trap presented by a trial, but it will also position us to be available to the Lord at any time, ready to respond to his will.

Unfortunately, the disciples did not watch and pray, and indeed, when a very severe trial came, they were completely unprepared. Not only did they not understand the trial, but they also responded to it in an inappropriate way and ultimately, abandoned their Lord. Jesus came back to them three times and found them asleep all three times.

Even though they had failed to watch and pray, and even though they were about to miserably fail the trial, Jesus continued to give them instructions, trying (unsuccessfully) to instruct and support them in his hour. "**Rise**! Let us go! Here comes my betrayer" (26:46). Jesus woke his disciples up and brought them together just before the soldiers and his betrayer arrived. He did his best to prepare them for what was about to happen. Instead, Peter thought Jesus wanted him to fight. When the men started to arrest Jesus, Peter "reached for his sword, drew it out and struck the servant of the high priest, cutting off his ear" (26:51). It's a good thing Jesus was not asking his disciples to fight. Peter was no doubt aiming for the man's head but instead cut off his ear.

After patiently healing the man-with-one-ear, Jesus again tried to instruct his disciples. "**Put** your sword back in its place...for all who draw the sword will die by the sword" (26:52). After all this time living with Jesus, following Jesus, listening to his word, and observing his works, his disciples did not even begin to understand the nature of the Kingdom of heaven. They still thought it was a human political arrangement, or perhaps a military dictatorship. They didn't see that the only thing violence can produce is more violence. They had no understanding of the divine nature of redemption, God bringing good out of bad, life out of death.

It's possible that even if these men had been consistently watching and praying, they would have still misunderstood the meaning and significance of that moment. But a watchful prayerfulness would have at least made them more attentive to the instructions of Jesus and more thoughtful about the best way to obey them.

"Then all the disciples deserted him and fled" (26:56).

Living a consistent yoked life is not a matter of fulfilling certain tasks in a certain way. It is a very personal, relational attentiveness to the Master. A faithful apprentice recognizes the role of the Master and seeks to serve and follow, no matter what the Master might need at the moment. While a certain amount of planning is good, in the end, a life of watchful prayer is ready to respond at a moment's notice. After all, a yoked person cannot really go anywhere or do anything without following the lead of the Strong One next to him.

"Watch and pray!"

10 SERMON ON THE END

I love how Matthew provided five groups of the teachings of Jesus. These five provided a clear sense of the nature of his message and mission, and they gave us the instructions needed to be faithful, productive citizens of his Kingdom.

The Sermon on the Mount beautifully taught the distinctive values of a greater righteousness and a deeper relationship that marked the rule of the Messiah and the lives of those committed to his rule. While recording instructions for the disciples, the Sermon on the Mission described the mission of God that had sent his Son to the earth, the mission that every representative of his Kingdom shares. The Sermon on the Kingdom painted wonderful pictures of the nature of the Messianic Kingdom, using stories Jesus taught as well as further explanations provided his disciples. Since Jesus was committed to building his Kingdom community, the Sermon on the Church raised the values that are to govern that community with wonderful promises of heaven's direct involvement.

The final group of teachings took place toward the end of the ministry of Jesus. The Sermon on the End began in the Temple area where Jesus had been teaching after his triumphal entry into Jerusalem (21:23). At the end, Jesus made clear, authoritative proclamations as the Prophet foretold by Moses (Deuteronomy 18:18). Jesus came to fulfill all the functions of Prophet, Priest and King. Jesus not only came to teach as the Great Rabbi, he also came to declare the Word of the Lord as the Great Prophet.

The Sermon on the End had two parts. The first part in the Temple area was the pronouncement of the Messiah of judgment on the generation that had rejected him and his mission. Jesus made a clear case for why the judgment of God was now necessary, why it was essential that God put an end to the religious system that opposed him and would ultimately lead to his death and the persecution of his followers. After leaving the Temple, Jesus continued teaching his disciples about the end, with a prophetic word concerning the pattern and final culmination of the end as well as important parables that gave instructions to his followers on their responsibility during this process. In some ways, the Sermon on the End provided a conclusion to the core teaching of Jesus in the Sermon on the Mount, just as the

Seven Woes provided a contrast to the Beatitudes.

Whenever we come to a passage of Scripture that addresses the end, either of an era or of human history, controversy always seems to break out. Everyone seems to have their favorite theory of the end, and there is no unity upon which theory is correct. This is certainly true of these teachings from Jesus, However, my focus is not on theology but rather on the commands of Jesus given in this teaching. It's vitally important to see that Jesus left his followers, including us, instructions for how to live during the last days. I'm of the view that the "last days" began with the resurrection of Jesus and will end with his return, so no matter when we may live, we are all in the last days. So, these final instructions are relevant to all of us, no matter what our favorite doctrinal "school" might be.

The Case for Judgment

The Old Testament prophets were called by God to call their generation to repentance as well as to announce future restoration. While they may not have liked it, some were called to be the official messengers of judgment. The "judgment of God" is not our favorite subject. To "judge" simply means "to separate." In the end, the need for God to judge is a simple recognition that a pattern of sin along with its consequences cannot be allowed to continue beyond a certain point. A time comes when sin and its consequences have to be stopped. To not do so would result in catastrophic death and destruction. The pattern of God's judgment is to allow sin to run its course in a generation or among a people. God doesn't punish a people as much as God allows the pattern of their sin to become its own kind of judgment. That has been true at different times, and among different people, and will be true one last time for all people. In the Sermon on the End, Jesus addressed both the need for judgment in his generation as well as the ultimate need for final judgment.

When an Old Testament prophet announced a message of judgment, he did so by making essentially a "legal" case for its necessity. God was committed to the need for a clear moral case, a convincing argument for the need for judgment. You can tell when a prophet was making such a case by the use of the word "Woe." When "woes" were pronounced by a prophet, each one was a point in their moral case. You can see examples of that in Isaiah (5:8, 11, 18, 20, 21, 22), Jeremiah (13:27; 22:13; 23:1), Ezekiel (13:3, 18; 16:23; 24:6), and Habakkuk (2:6, 9, 12, 15, 19). Now, in the Sermon on the End, we see Jesus doing the same thing. He began by making the case for judgment by publicly pronouncing seven "Woes" in the Temple area. He followed up with a prophecy of the end and parables that provided instructions for those living in the end   – for all of us.

Jesus began by addressing the crowds and the disciples. In his day, the Scribes and the Pharisees were attempting to carry on the tradition established by Moses, to be faithful to remind the people of the Law of Moses. While they may have accurately quoted Moses, their hypocrisy communicated a very different message. Jesus emphasized this point with a series of important commands. "So you must **be careful** to **do** everything they tell you. But do not **do** what they do, for they do not practice what they preach" (23:3). Merely knowing what the Law said was not sufficient. It was essential that the citizens of God's Kingdom practice the heart and spirit of the Law. Knowing without doing just added up to hypocrisy.

As hypocrites, the Scribes and Pharisees focused on appearing pious, and in that way, demanding honor and privilege from the others in society. They did this in a variety of ways.

Heavy yokes. While Jesus had declared that his yoke was easy and his burden was light, the yoke of the religious leaders was heavy and burdensome. Not only did they make harsh demands on those attempting to follow their teaching, they did nothing to assist them in their walk.

Phylacteries and tassels. A focus on external religion resulted in a contest to see who could have the most noticeable, visible evidence of personal piety. "Tassels" actually had their origin in the Law of Moses (Numbers 15:37-41; Deuteronomy 22:12). They were blue cords worn at the corner of garments, visible reminders of the need to obey the commandments of the Lord. "Phylacteries" were small leather boxes containing small pieces of papers with Exodus 13:1-16; Deuteronomy 6:4-6; and Deuteronomy 11:13-21 written on them. While the Lord had commanded the people to tie the Law as symbols on the people's hands and foreheads (Deuteronomy 6:8), the religious leaders of the day decided to make the phylacteries as wide as possible and the tassels as long as possible in order to draw maximum attention to themselves.

Places of honor and important seats. As is even true in some cultures today, seating arrangements were designed to reflect status and significance. The religious leaders wanted to make sure their importance was always obvious to all.

Titles of honor. It's only natural to address others in a respectful manner. However, the religious leaders insisted on being addressed in a way that reflected their honor and privilege in society. Because the citizens of the Kingdom of Heaven were all brothers and sisters, an insistence on being honored above another was contrary to the spirit and values of the Kingdom. The Scribes and Pharisees were attention-grabbers and status-seekers. On the other hand, the highest value in the Kingdom was placed on being a servant, and on taking the humble place among others.

"The greatest among you will be your servant. For those who exalt themselves will be humbled, and those who humble themselves will be exalted" (23:11-12). Jesus declared that the religionists that focused on gaining honor for themselves would, of necessity, be humbled, setting the stage for his specific case against them, calling for judgment.

First Woe

Jesus stated his prophetic case by once again addressing the central concern about hypocrisy. The Scribes (the teachers of the Law) and the Pharisees, were actually blocking the way into the Kingdom of heaven. Because of their insistence on their own traditions, misinterpreting and misapplying God's revelation in the Old Testament, those they were influencing did not have a true understanding of God or of God's righteous rule. And because they opposed Jesus, the King who was announcing and inaugurating the Kingdom of heaven in their generation, they were blocking any effort on the part of those who would have otherwise accepted the message and the invitation of Jesus.

Second Woe

Jesus then declared that these same Scribes and Pharisees, in their zeal to make converts to their religious system, were producing even more rigid, fanatical legalists. In fact, Jewish converts outside of Israel were often more violently opposed to faith in Jesus than their Jewish teachers. While visiting Jerusalem, Paul was confronted by Jewish converts from Asia who started a riot when they saw him in the temple area (Acts 21:27-28). While the Scribes and Pharisees were blocking entrance into the Kingdom, their converts were openly and violently opposing it.

Third Woe

The third issue is one that Jesus addressed in the Sermon on the Mount (5:33-37). Legalism as a religious system is all about "building a wall around the law" in order to make it more specific, and ultimately, to provide loopholes or ways around it. The way the religious leaders taught the issue of taking oaths was a typical case. Rather than a simple understanding of the need for honesty and integrity, knowing that God takes our word as sacred, they established a system of oaths so that some would carry less importance than others. Not all had legal force, and some even contradicted the Law (for example, the principle of Corban in Mark 7:11-13). In this case, the Pharisees taught that only oaths based on the name and attributes of God, as well as gifts dedicated to the temple, were binding. Jesus pointed out the absurdity of this reasoning, concluding that "anyone who swears by heaven swears by God's throne and by the one who sits on it" (23:22). The honesty of a person's words was always an issue in God's eyes. Teaching a religious rationale for dishonesty could not be tolerated.

Fourth Woe

Jesus then judged the hypocrisy of the religious leaders in another way. It was the custom of the worshipers in Jesus' day to tithe a portion of their primary crops, but the Pharisees wanted to seem even more scrupulous than the common, godly folks of the day. They made a point of saying that not only did they tithe their crops, they even tithed the spices grown in their gardens. On the other hand, their legalistic, religious lifestyles completely neglected things like justice, mercy and faithfulness, core values of God's Kingdom. They had forgotten the clear statement of the prophet Micah: "What does the Lord require of you? To act justly and to love mercy and to walk humbly with your God" (6:8). The religious practices of the Scribes and Pharisees maybe resulted in their looking very pious in the eyes of some, but they resulted in the exact opposite of the virtues God was requiring of them.

Fifth Woe

A fifth aspect of the religious play-acting of the Scribes and Pharisees was an overall emphasis on externals. Their teaching led people to believe that looking good on the outside, conforming to external signs of piety, was the primary thing. Holiness was a matter of outward appearance. However, on the inside their lives were "full of greed and self-indulgence." It's not uncommon to find that teachers and preachers who focus on external conformity to religious rules can, over time, prove to have significant moral failures in their private lives, a fact that will eventually become visible.

Jesus emphasized this important insight by making clear, authoritative commands. "Blind Pharisee! First **clean** the inside of the cup and dish, and then the outside also be clean" (23:26). What is in the heart of a person is the core issue.

Finding a place of freedom and purity in the heart is what God values and offers. However, when a person experiences transformation of heart and mind, evidences of it will be visible as well.

Sixth Woe

Jesus then compared the Scribes and Pharisees to whitewashed tombs. Before a festival that would be attended by people from outside of Israel, the local folks whitewashed the outside of the tombs. Their purpose was to make clear which areas had human remains in them, so they could be avoided. Even accidentally touching a dead body would result in "uncleanness," keeping a visitor from participating in the festival. The white on the entrance of tombs maybe looked good, but it's significance was the very opposite. In the same way, the religious hypocrites perhaps looked righteous on the outside, but in reality, "on the inside you are full of hypocrisy and wickedness" (23:28). Even though they professed a zeal for the Law, doing everything they could to give the right religious appearance, their hearts were filled with lawlessness.

Seventh Woe

Finally, Jesus condemned the Scribes and Pharisees for the hypocrisy of decorating the graves of martyred prophets from the past, claiming that they were more righteous than their ancestors who had killed the prophets. However, Jesus made it clear that these religious leaders were the descendants of those who had committed such atrocities in the past. They were cut from the same cloth. Their claim to greater righteousness was a fraud!

These seven prophetic pronouncements of judgment were simply examples of a religious system that misrepresented God and opposed the announcement and coming of God's Kingdom. For that reason, it was now clear that judgment upon that generation was morally required. Jesus began to clearly describe the judgment to come by drawing an authoritative conclusion from the seventh woe. "Go ahead, then, and **complete** what your ancestors started" (23:32). The generation that opposed the coming of their Messiah and his righteous rule, would fulfill all the lawlessness of past generations, and suffer the necessary consequences.

"How will you escape being condemned to hell?" (23:33). We may be more comfortable hearing the words of Rabbi Jesus than the declarations of Jesus the Prophet, but who was more qualified than Jesus to make an official pronouncement of judgment. After all, the Father has appointed Jesus "to judge the world with justice" (Acts 17:31).

As was true with former generations who shed righteous blood, the generation of religious leaders Jesus was addressing would, in the future, "kill...and flog...and pursue" those Jesus would send to continue his mission. For that reason, judgment for all the righteous bloodshed in past generations would come upon that generation. "Your house is left to you desolate" (23:38).

It reminds me of a picture painted by the old prophets of a "cup of God's wrath" (see for example Jeremiah 25:15, and Revelation 14:10). The prophets proposed that every nation – people or generation – added to their own cup of sin and iniquity, and if there was never a time of repentance, of turning to the Lord, eventually it would be possible for that cup to fill up, and even overflow. When the cup of iniquity overflowed, it became a "cup of wrath" and judgment was the result. In essence, Jesus was saying that the cup of lawlessness and hypocrisy was about to overflow in that generation of religious leaders in judgment.

But don't think that Jesus enjoyed announcing judgment. Sometimes we think that prophets have to be harsh and unfeeling in order to speak hard words to a people. Actually, the opposite is true. If a prophet speaks a hard word harshly, they are not representing the heart of God. All prophets who announced judgment did so weeping.

The same was true of Jesus. "How often I wanted to gather your children together, the way a hen gathers her chicks under her wings, and you were unwilling" (23:38). Luke's account recorded the moment this way: "As he...saw the city, he wept over it" (19:41). The heart of Jesus was to bring redemption and restoration to his generation, and he provided every opportunity, in his teaching and ministry, to do so. It's also true that every prophecy of judgment included a prophecy of future hope. "You will not see me again until you say, 'Blessed is he who comes in the name of the Lord'" (Matthew 23:38). Before the end, God's people will welcome their Messiah.

Signs of Judgment

The teaching of Jesus in chapter 24 makes you wonder whether or not the disciples really understood what had just happened in the temple area. The pronouncement of judgment by Jesus would have a profound effect on temple worship. Their house of worship would be left "desolate." But the disciples couldn't see beyond their pride in the beauty of the house that still stood before them, taking time to draw the attention of Jesus to the impressive structures. For that reason, it was necessary for Jesus to take the time to be more explicit about the nature and process of judgment that was to come.

In fact, the tendency to misunderstand the teaching of Jesus concerning the process of the coming of his Kingdom in history and the culmination and end of that process is frequently misunderstood. Everyone has their favorite view of how this age of redemption, this "church age," will progress and be brought to a conclusion. Those views tend to be either overly optimistic or overly pessimistic, depending on the cultural mood of the moment. Today's Jesus followers either prefer a dream of a theocracy established by the church to bring in a "kingdom age," or to see everything burning up in defeat, making any commitment to the mission of God in the world a fool's errand. And the views of the "Olivet Discourse" in Matthew 24 are at the heart of these varying views. However, my purpose is to explore the "commands," the imperatives found in this teaching, and the practical applications Jesus intended for his followers in every generation.

First, Jesus had to get the disciples' minds off of their focus on the splendor of the temple buildings. "Not one stone here will be left on another; everyone will be thrown down" (24:2). The temple buildings they took so much pride in were temporary features at best, and in fact, judgment would result in the destruction of those buildings. The full establishment of the Kingdom of heaven on earth that would include a process of judgment would result in permanent structures that would far outshine anything they had seen.

This statement finally got the attention of the disciples and they wanted to know more. They asked Jesus two questions: "When will this happen?" and "What will be the sign of your coming and of the end of the age?" I'm impressed by the fact that the disciples at least seemed to understand that the end of the age had everything to do with the coming, the return of Jesus. There could be no Kingdom without a King.

Jesus began by giving them a first command. "**Watch out** that no one deceives you" (24:4). Deception is the primary strategy of the enemy, clever attempts to distract and mislead the followers of Jesus. Somehow deceptive strategies would focus on views of the end. It would be possible to be so focused on a theory of the end, a primary focus on King Jesus and his righteous rule in every place and time would be neglected. They were to be alert to these strategies and to "keep the main thing the main thing," to keep their eyes on Jesus, no matter how upsetting circumstances might be.

Attempts to distract and mislead the disciples would include claims from false Messiahs. There would also be attempts to frighten the disciples, to get them to focus on negative aspects of the historical outworking of the Kingdom. This gave rise to a second command. "You will hear of wars and rumors of wars, but **see to it** that you are not alarmed. Such things must happen, but the end is still to come" (24:6). The "last days," the time between the first coming and the return of Christ, would be a time of overlapping kingdoms in conflict with each other, resulting in times of stress and trouble. That reality should not surprise or discourage the alert, prepared followers of Jesus.

Jesus provided a fairly detailed description of the war between the kingdoms. Commentators have long debated whether or not Jesus was prophesying about the destruction of the temple and the city of Jerusalem in A.D. 70, or the final conflict at the end of the age. I think such "either/or" thinking runs the risk of missing the point. It was not uncommon for the Old Testament prophets to make pronouncements that we sometimes refer to in terms of "double reference/double fulfillment." The prophets didn't always see the outworking of God's purpose in a straight line, but saw highlights and key, sometimes repeatable patterns. Every generation has wanted to think they were the last generation. So far, each one has been wrong. It's more helpful to see Jesus describing a pattern of conflict, one that will certainly come to an end at some point in time. And while describing that pattern, Jesus made very important statements that are meaningful to every generation.

For example, "the one who stands firm to the end will be saved" (24:13). The word translated "stands firm" is a favorite term in the New Testament whenever conflict and persecution was being addressed. It was most often translated "persevere," and simply meant to endure, literally to "abide under." It described someone who refused to give up under pressure, who refused to give ground to the enemy. To that end, deliverance will come to the one who sticks to it and refuses to quit.

My favorite promise in this passage is found in verse 14. "And this gospel of the kingdom will be preached in the whole world as a testimony to all nations." The Gospel will prevail! The preaching of the Gospel will triumph! The Good News of the Messianic reign of God, coming from heaven to earth, will reach the whole world! Then and only then, "the end will come." Those who take a more pessimistic view of the way this age winds down tend to be too quick to want to just get out of here. Let the world go to hell in a hand basket! However, the primary concern of every committed Jesus follower is the powerful preaching of the Gospel to every nation of the world. It's possible for every generation to simply admit, "We still have work to do!"

The prophecy of Jesus in Matthew 24 drew heavily upon the prophecy of Daniel chapter 7. Frankly, there is a long history of disagreement on specifically what Daniel was prophesying and how it was to be fulfilled. It's no wonder Jesus gave another command in this context. "**Let the reader understand**" (24:15.). Careful thought, and consideration is recommended. Don't jump to conclusions. Seek and wait for true understanding. Don't miss the point!

There will be times when the conflict between the Kingdom of God and the kingdom of the world will result in extreme instability. It will be a dangerous time, calling for intense spiritual focus and understanding. It's in the context of that kind of time that Jesus gave another command. "**Pray**" (24:20). Pray for the grace and wisdom of God to be provided during those times. Drawing close to the Lord in an attitude of humble dependence will be essential. These times call for a moment-by-moment listening ear and obedient heart. Once again, Jesus drew attention to the deception of false messiahs, even some would be "miracle workers." The best strategy is to keep your eyes on Jesus, for when Jesus returns, there will be no wondering about it. Everyone will see and know.

Beginning in verse 29 Jesus used the words of the prophet Isaiah (13:10; 34:4) to speak of a final conflict and the culmination of the entire process of the Messianic Kingdom being established on the earth, a process that would require the elimination of every other kingdom.

The great drama of the end would be followed by another authoritative instruction. "Now **learn** this lesson from the fig tree" (24:32). The various signs spoken of by Jesus must be interpreted correctly by his followers. While many of the signs are repeatable throughout the church age, there will be a final sign, a final conflict, the culmination and restoration of all things. Having ears to hear throughout the process is essential. Let the Word of God guide us, for "heaven and earth will pass away, but my words will never pass away" (24:35).

You'll remember that the disciples asked about the signs of the end. They also asked about the time. They maybe didn't like the answer Jesus now gave. "But about that day or hour no one knows, nor the Son, but only the Father" (24:36). I remember the uproar caused once when I recommended the book, "Ninety-nine reasons why no one knows when Christ will return," to the church book store. For some reason, it seems important for us to know, even though Jesus was clear that no one would know. In fact, Jesus seemed to think that his return would be a necessary surprise. Many will be going about their normal business, ignoring the call to repent and seek the Kingdom. Somehow, it's essential that we not know, neither is it possible to predict, the time of the Lord's return.

Perhaps it's our desire to be in control of our future that makes us so invested in predicting the end of the world. But Jesus does not want us to be in control, he wants us to trust, to stay close, and stay alert.

Parables of the End

Rather than attempting to offer support to any system of end-time doctrine, I'm more interested in the bottom line. What were the take-aways Jesus wanted us to grasp? What were the authoritative instructions Jesus gave in his teaching, the commands that he wanted us to obey.

Jesus followed up his prophetic announcement of judgment and his teaching about the process leading up to the end by giving four very important parables. As was often true in the teachings of Jesus, his parables provided vitally important pictures of truth, of the core of the message he was communicating. Understanding the important point of the parable not only connects us with the point of the teaching but of the needed response.

Faithful and Wicked Servants

The first parable is found in verses 42-51. This first parable provides a very clear statement about what we should learn from the previous statement. In fact, there are three important commands in the introduction of this parable.

"Therefore **keep watch,** because you do not know on what day your Lord will come" (24:42). What Jesus called for was not a secret ability to predict the time of his return but rather of spiritual watchfulness. An intentional alertness, a sensitivity to the word of God, the ability to discern the Holy Spirit's movements, will be essential throughout the "last days," and especially at the end. If it were possible to predict the time specifically, this kind of alertness would not be needed. However, since the Father is in complete control of the timing, the task of the disciples of Jesus is to be on the alert at all times.

"But **understand** this: If the owner of the house had known at what time of night the thief was coming, he would have kept watch and would not have let his house be broken into" (24:43). Jesus emphasized the need to be clear about this. If it were possible to know the timing of the return of Jesus exactly, watchfulness would only be needed just before that time. However, Jesus was calling for a lifestyle of spiritual alertness.

"So you also must **be ready**, because the Son of Man will come at an hour when you do not expect him" (24:44). A constant state of readiness is expected of those who are committed to responsible citizenship in the Messiah's Kingdom.

There are so many distractions in life, so many things that draw our attention away from the work and progress of the Kingdom. Staying alert, being ready, requires a high level of commitment, one that Jesus was commanding in this parable. "Therefore" makes it clear that this point is the response Jesus is looking for at the end of his teaching on the end.

Jesus then provided an illustration in the Parable of the Faithful and Wicked Servants. The Master of the household had charged his servants with providing food for the household, and would expect them to be faithfully doing so when he returned. It's possible, however, for a wicked servant to conclude that the Master was going to be gone a very long time, and so he could get away with being unfaithful. So unfaithful that he would begin to abuse the members of the household and live carelessly. What he didn't count on was the inevitability of the Master returning unexpectedly. And when he does, finding the servant being unfaithful and irresponsible, there would be severe consequences. It was simple carelessness that led the servant down the wrong path. "Therefore keep watch."

Wise and Foolish Bridesmaids

Jesus then taught two kingdom parables. We saw a wonderful series of kingdom parables in chapter 13, but here Jesus added two more pertaining to the process leading up to and preparation for the end.

It's amazing how many theories have been suggested (and preached) about the meaning of the parable of the wise and foolish virgins. Many view the parable as teaching the difference between those born again and those not born again, or even the difference between those who are Spirit filled and those not Spirit filled. However, when Jesus taught this parable, he had not died and risen from the dead so salvation by grace through faith in the resurrected Christ was not yet a reality and the Day of Pentecost had not yet come. This was a simple story that would have connected easily and naturally with those listeners.

In the first century, Jewish wedding ceremonies took place over a seven-day period. The ceremonies had two distinct companies: the groom and his company and the bride and her bridesmaids. The bridesmaids were all young women between the ages of 12 and 18. On the first night of the wedding, the groom and his company were to parade to the bride's home in order to formally escort her back to the groom's home. It was the task of the bridesmaids to meet the groom and company halfway to join in the parade. However, there was no set schedule for all of this to take place.

And so, this parable of the Kingdom uses a story about a wedding ceremony to make a very important point. Jesus referred to five of the ten bridesmaids as wise while the other five were foolish. The difference between them was the level of preparedness demonstrated by the wise. They not only brought lamps to light the way, they also brought a jar of oil in case the groom's company came later than expected. The foolish only brought their lamps and no extra oil.

Sure enough, the groom's company took their time and showed up with their parade late into the evening. By then, the oil in the lamps had run out, so it was only those who had brought extra oil with them that were able to join in the parade.

Now, we may consider the seeming lack of compassion on the part of the wise bridesmaids to be questionable. However, Jesus was not teaching a parable about compassion. To make that clear, Jesus gave a command when stating the conclusion of the parable. "Therefore **keep watch**, because you do not know the day or the hour" (25:13). The issue was once again the need for personal and spiritual watchfulness and alertness. The need is for faithfulness and preparedness, preparedness being a life of obedience to God. And those who are ready are counted as wise.

Fruitful and Lazy Servants

"Again," shows this next parable to also be a Kingdom parable and related to the one just taught. This parable tells the story of three servants who were entrusted with a part of their Master's wealth as stewards. As with the Parable of Faithful and Wicked Servants above, the lesson to be learned is really quite simple and clear: being alert and prepared includes being faithful. The issue is stewardship, the responsibility for wise, faithful, and productive management of the Lord's gifts provided his servants.

These three servants were each given a "bag of gold," or literally a "talent." In Matthew chapter 18 we saw that a "talent" was 75 to 100 pounds of silver or gold. It was basically a million dollars. The three servants in the parable were given one million, two million and five million dollars to manage for their Master, "each according to his ability" (25:15). The Master not only provided the gold, he had also provided a certain kind of ability or capability to manage that amount of gold. It was fully recognized that each manager had a unique skill-set, a unique gift-mix, that corresponded to a realistic expectation of what he/she was potentially able to do with all that gold. "To whom much is given, much is required!"

The Master "went on a journey," trusting the three managers to be faithful with what they had been given. The one with the five bags of gold and the one with the two bags immediately went to work with the intention of making a productive use of what they had been entrusted with. However, the one with "only" one million dollars, rather than giving himself to productive work, chose to dig a hole in the ground and bury his bag.

"After a long time," the Master returned and received a report of his managers' stewardship. Both the one with the five million and the one with the two million dollars reported a 100% return on the resources entrusted to them. The response of the Master is crucial to our understanding and application of this parable. "Well done, good and faithful servant! You have been faithful with a few things; I will put you in charge of many things. Come and share your master's happiness!" (verses 21 and 23).

First of all, these two servants were commended for being "good and faithful." The criteria the Master used to judge them was their good heart and faithful service. There were really no other "metrics," just faithfulness. They weren't rewarded based on their influence or personal accomplishments, just on their faithfulness to the Master and the stewardship he had entrusted them.

Second, a promise of eternal reward was given. Based on their faithfulness, each of these two managers were promised that they would be put "in charge of many things." Their faithful, productive stewardship would result in increasing opportunities to continue being faithful and productive in ever increasing ways. A growing pattern of assigned responsibilities is an important aspect of faithful stewardship.

Finally, each servant received the same core reward. Each one was allowed to "Come and share your master's happiness." Entering into the joy of the Master, a joy found in his immediate presence, is the greatest reward imaginable. And it is a reward infinitely valuable to those who are primarily motivated by a desire to be with the Master.

However, the servant with one bag of gold had a very different perspective. When he gave his report to the Master he began by expressing a harsh opinion of the Master's character and motivation. "I knew that you are a hard man, harvesting where you have not sown and gathering where you have not scattered seed" (25:24). This translation doesn't really do justice to the expression and attitude of this servant. "Hard" literally referred to someone who was harsh, cruel and merciless. Someone who was only interested in exploiting others for personal benefit. "Reaping where you have not sown" is a description of someone who robs other people's harvest for himself without consideration for the well-being of the one who had done all the work. In other words, this servant was accusing the Master of being a vicious tyrant who took whatever he wanted, not caring for those he took from.

As a result, this servant reported that he had hid his bag of gold in a hole in the ground. He had made no attempt to manage the resource in a faithful and productive way.

Instead of describing this servant as good and faithful, he was described as evil and lazy. An evil heart instead of a good heart described someone who was entirely self-centered, concerned with short-term personal benefits and not the benefits that would go to others, either in the short or the long term. It was a heart set on self-indulgence, self-gratification, and self-promotion. In fact, if this servant had been the Master, he would no doubt have been the kind of master he was accusing his master of being. "Lazy" referred to someone who was often idle and troublesome, someone who would find the need for faithful and productive work too much bother.

If this last servant had been only lazy, and not also evil, he would have thought to deposit the one million dollars in a bank so it could at least earn some kind of interest!

As a result of his evil heart and lazy attitude, this servant's bag of gold was to be given to the one who started with five and ended up with ten bags of gold. The idea of progressive productivity as a result of consistent faithfulness was once again the lesson to be learned. And the evil, lazy servant? He was to be separated from the

Master. After all, he never really wanted to be in vital, personal relationship with the Master to begin with.

Being alert and ready, being watchful and prepared, includes being faithful and productive, with a good heart and a personal commitment to serving the Master. A posture of an evil, self-focused life and a commitment to a careless approach to life will result in a complete lack of readiness for the Master's return. After all, such a person is not really looking or longing for that return.

Blessed and Cursed Nations

Jesus taught one more parable, this one a picture of final judgment at the end of it all. The message is similar to the Parable of the Weeds (13:24-30) and the Parable of the Net (13:47-52). Because Jesus described the basis (at least in part) for the judgment he will eventually pronounce, we can also draw conclusions about the Kingdom values that are in the heart of the King and that will be finally established when all is said and done.

The way Jesus introduced this final parable makes the context clear. "When the Son of Man comes in his glory, and all the angels with him, he will sit on his glorious throne" (25:31). No matter what your favorite theory about the end and how it will unfold, this is clearly a picture of King Jesus taking his place on the throne of all God has made, to rule for eternity. The kingdom of the world is being fully displaced by the Kingdom of God.

The final judgment is described in terms of a major separation, separating people "as a shepherd separates the sheep from the goats." All are human beings, but the shepherd's sheep are given a place of honor, at the shepherd's right hand, while the goats, now fully separated from the sheep, must find their place on his left hand.

The first pronouncement concerns the sheep, and describes both the nature and the basis for their eternal reward. "Come, you who are blessed by my Father" (25:34). These are the blessed described in the Beatitudes, those who have the favor of the Father resting on them. "Take your inheritance." They are receiving their place in God's eternal Kingdom, their true inheritance as citizens of God's Kingdom and members of God's Household. "...the Kingdom prepared for you since the creation of the world." Somehow, God has been preparing this eternal inheritance from the beginning. This is what God always had in mind, an inheritance that had been interrupted by humanity's decision to come out from under God's righteous rule. And it's not so much an inheritance that has been earned as it is an inheritance that had been planned by God all along.

The King then described the characteristics of his sheep. These statements confirmed the fact that they had been living out the core values of the Kingdom. They had been living according to the Law of Love that had always been at the heart of God's moral character. They demonstrated that love by actively showing mercy and compassion to those in need.

Specifically, they had shown mercy by (1) Providing food to the hungry; (2) Providing drink to the thirsty; (3) Showing hospitality to strangers; (4) Providing clothes to those who needed them; (5) Caring for the sick; and (6) Visiting those in prison. Where there was a need for compassionate care, the shepherd's sheep could be found.

When the sheep are seen questioning when the Shepherd had seen them doing these acts of mercy, his reply formed the heart of the message being taught in this parable. "Truly I tell you, whatever you did for one of the least of these of these brothers and sisters of mine, you did it for me" (25:40). "Truly I tell you" was an "Amen saying," literally, "Amen, I say to you," emphasizing that the statement to follow was especially important. It referred to any time someone had humbly served a person in need, including (if not especially) "one of the least of these." This literally referred to "one of the little ones," a word used by Jesus in his teaching about the church (18:6, 10, 14). It is the service of those who are unable to offer any kind of a reward, to those who are weak and vulnerable, even invisible in the surrounding culture, that catches the attention of the Shepherd.

"...you did it for me." The Shepherd was in complete solidarity, identifying himself fully, with the weak ones, the defenseless ones, the ones who would be neglected if not for the compassionate service of the sheep who represented and lived out the heart and values of the Shepherd. It reminds me of the time Jesus confronted Saul of Tarsus and asked him, "Why do you persecute me?" (Acts 9:4). Jesus fully identified himself with those believers Saul was persecuting as if he had been personally persecuting Jesus. The heart of the Shepherd is now seen as a controlling factor in the final judgment.

On the other hand, the goats are judged for failing to live out of the core values of the Kingdom. Instead of humble compassion and mercy these goats lived solely for their own benefit, promoting their own self-interest, serving themselves. "Whatever you did not do for one of the least of these, you did not do for me"

(25:45). If they had been in relationship with the Shepherd, if they had made any attempt to follow the Shepherd or to participate in the Shepherd's mission, they would not have lived a self-absorbed life, a life contrary to the heart and nature of the Shepherd. As John wrote, "God is love," and that love is all about self-giving and humble serving, serving those who may be invisible to others, but a way God sees.

Those being judged are "all the nations." While these Kingdom characteristics are certainly relevant to individuals, even the nations will be judged by how they treated others, either with compassion or governed by self-interest. It also seems clear that those Jesus followers who suffer persecution at the hands of these nations are in view, both rewarding those who are merciful to them and judging those who are not.

In the end, there are two eternal homes. One is with the Father and the King, a home filled with perfect love, perfect peace, and complete joy. The other is filled with selfishness and self-interest. Every human person will end up spending eternity in the home of their choice.

And so, we end where we began.

"All authority in heaven and on earth has been given to me. Therefore go and **make disciples** of all nations, baptizing them in the name of the Father and of the Son and of the Holy Spirit, and teaching them to obey everything I have commanded you. And surely I am with you always, to the very end of the age" (28:18-20).

We are blessed, happy followers of the King and fellow participants of the King's mission. And we have been commissioned, we have been commanded, to be faithful and fruitful stewards of our particular assignment in the mission. Our heart is to hear and obey, so let us go forth to love and serve the Lord in our generation! Amen!

ABOUT THE AUTHOR

Larry Asplund is the son and the father of a pastor, coming from a long line of Christian ministers and educators. He has been in pastoral leadership and teaching in higher education for 51 years, serving as an associate pastor, teaching pastor, senior pastor, and church planter, as well as a Bible college teacher, seminary teacher, and University Vice President. He was married to his best friend and ministry partner, Lynda Sutton Asplund, for 47 years, before she Graduated to Glory in June of 2018. Larry and Lynda have two wonderful adult children and four very interesting grandsons. Larry has earned a B.A. in Biblical Studies, M.A. in Biblical Literature, and D.Min. in Leadership and Spiritual Formation.

www.ingramcontent.com/pod-product-compliance
Lightning Source LLC
LaVergne TN
LVHW041224080426
835508LV00011B/1069